D1717339

Sven Damm

Event Management:
How to Apply Best Practices
to Small Scale Events

Diplomica® Verlag GmbH

**Damm, Sven: Event Management: How to Apply Best Practices to Small Scale Events.
Hamburg, Diplomica Verlag GmbH 2011**

ISBN: 978-3-8428-5130-6
Druck: Diplomica® Verlag GmbH, Hamburg, 2011

Bibliografische Information der Deutschen Nationalbibliothek:
Die Deutsche Nationalbibliothek verzeichnet diese Publikation in der Deutschen
Nationalbibliografie; detaillierte bibliografische Daten sind im Internet über
http://dnb.d-nb.de abrufbar.

Die digitale Ausgabe (eBook-Ausgabe) dieses Titels trägt die ISBN 978-3-8428-0130-1
und kann über den Handel oder den Verlag bezogen werden.

© Diplomica Verlag GmbH
http://www.diplomica-verlag.de, Hamburg 2011
Printed in Germany

Abstract

Event management is a ubiquitous word in modern society. The word is used for small business breakfasts, large corporate shows and also for big international sport events, such as the Olympic Games. We all have an idea of what management is, but what is an event?

An event is often described as something that 'happens', and therefore, in that sense, we could use the term event management to describe the organisation of everything that happens. Getz defines an event as 'an occurrence at a given place; a special set of circumstances; a noteworthy occurrence'(Getz, 2007, p. 18), and this definition embraces a wide range of possibilities with one important thing in common: they can only occur once. As such, one key characteristic of events is that they are not continuous, for they each have a beginning and an end, and every event is different from the last one. "No matter how hard one tries, it is literally impossible to replicate an event" (Getz, 2007, p. 18); thus, when watching the Olympic Games, we do not see the same picture repeating itself every four years, for the event changes and evolves over time. Consequently, to fully understand how things happen within any given event, it is necessary to get involved in the planning and execution of an event.

Malhotra writes that events are an important aspect of human life and that our understanding of them is poorly developed. He thinks that there is a "need to enhance the understanding of the subject" (Malhotra, 2002, p. 179), and this opinion is supported by the relative youth of academic study into the topic. In their book, 'Festival & Special Event Management', Allen, O'Toole, Harris and McDonnell (2008) date the birth of the industry to the 1980s, where "several seminal events set the pattern for the contemporary event industry as we know it today" (Allen et al., 2008, p. 9). Thus, especially compared with other disciplines in the field of social science, event management is a young discipline, and there is not yet a huge base of research to work with. In addition, rather than academically rigorous research conducted by professional researchers, much of the knowledge in the field has been generated by practising event managers who have written books about their own experiences, knowledge, and skills (Allen et al., 2008; Catherwood & Van Kirk, 1992; Getz, 2007; Goldblatt, 1997)

It is of no surprise that these practitioners, and the events they discuss, tend to reflect the planning of the biggest events the earth has seen, such as the Olympic Games and US presidential inaugurations. These authors possess a great deal of experience, and their past involvement has generated a variety of different ideas about what constitutes best practice in event management. Consequently, the literature concentrates on events that change not only the local community, but also influence a broad variety of people on earth, from international participants and spectators through to TV broadcasting and internet coverage.

Getz reinforces the distinction between academic researcher and front-line practitioner, commenting that only a few event managers write about their experiences: 'Speaking as a journal editor, I can say that it has proved close to impossible to get practitioners to contribute research papers or case studies to the refereed, academic literature. The starting point is for practitioners to be reflective, not just focused on the task at hand, and to use this reflection in part to initiate research projects' (Getz, 2007, p. 354). Getz emphasises that the ties between practitioners and academics are currently loose, and that the field of event management could be significantly improved by both sectors working more closely together.

Ultimately, this book combines a range of differing views about best practice and recommended behaviours; it identifies and recommends an event management model that potentially enables small-scale event managers to fully develop the potential of such events. This book reduces the gap between theory and practice and the framework of best practices can be applied to significantly improve the quality of management similar events in the future.

Table of Content

List of Tables and Figure

1. Introduction and Context

1.1 Overview

Events have been around forever. The word *'event'* is derived from the Latin word *'eventus'* and was originally used to describe big happenings out of the ordinary ("Event," 2009) Today, the concept of events includes a large variety of social gatherings, meetings, sports, shows, and performances. It has become a fashion to use the word *'event'* for everything that is happening.

In recent years, the number of events has grown rapidly and an industry around events has evolved. This event industry has seen significant growth over the last three decades, which has made it hard to complete an overview of all the facets of events and event management. While several companies in this growing trade have good organizational structures and management processes in place, a rather confusing picture evolves when looking at the entire event industry. Nevertheless, despite that confusing structure remaining in place, the International Special Events Society (ISES) states that the event industry is still one of the world's fastest growing, economically-lucrative industries, while *"in the Western World most of the benefits have been squeezed out of process improvement and neoclassical economics"* (Clifton, 2009).

Indeed, the world has been hit hard by the financial crisis of 2008-2009, and many businesses have failed because they had already optimized their processes and were not able to cut down costs to match the lack of international demand. However, a focus on the optimization of internal processes, and a consequent lack of any new business ideas over the past 25 years (Clifton, 2009), is a phenomenon that appears to have passed by the event management industry. Until this crisis, the event industry had not been interested in optimizing its processes nor in utilising its full potential and most businesses in this industry has managed to survive by focusing on cost-saving strategies and opportunities to attract new customers.

Perhaps because of this rather unique status in the modern business world, the field of event management does not include an existing structure of literature that researchers can build upon as a foundation for their work. A scan of the limited literature that does exist highlights a wide range of contrary opinions and the absence of agreed definition, while most research so far has been focused on the description of specific events and on explanation of observations made during that event. Thus, though several authors have mentioned the need for a framework of best practices in event management (William J. O'Toole, 2000; Silvers, Bowdin, O'Toole, & Nelson, 2006), no such framework has yet proven to be sustainable. One consequence of this lack of framework is that it is difficult or even impossible to improve event practitioner performance and to evaluate the people working in the business against any global benchmark. As a result, event management is not given serious consideration as a profession, and it is therefore difficult for the industry to achieve international acknowledgement and reputation.

While event managers working with large scale events can still achieve international recognition for their work, managers of small scale local events do not have any such opportunity, and it is this present status that the current research attempts to investigate. This book sets out to explore whether, and how, small scale event managers can improve their performance by using a framework of best practice in event management derived from a range of different sources. The findings, discussion, and recommendations contained in this book have resulted from analysis of the strengths and weaknesses of each contributing source, and ultimately propose a framework of best practice in event management for small scale local event managers that will assist those managers to enhance the quality of experience for event participants while taking better advantage of growth opportunities for their firms.

This is particularly important because the majority of events around the world are small scale local events, and better usage of their potential could lead to a boost in industry growth that will create economic benefits for the event, the community, and the country. The original research described in this book was conducted in New Zealand, a country that has a large variety of small scale events, especially in the tourism sector. This sector is of special interest, as the Rugby World Cup of 2011 will be held in New Zealand and a spectrum of small-scale events will be launched to support this international event. For New Zealand, this is a promising opportunity to generate long term benefits for the entire country through the creation of numerous world class though small-scale events around one big 'magnet' event. For this reason alone, it seems worthwhile to conduct research in the field of small-scale event management, in order to determine what constitutes success factors for this industry.

1.2 Research Question

The central question that forms the basis for this research is:

To what extent does a theoretical best practices framework, for the effective management of mega-events, provide optimum guidance for the management of small-scale local events in New Zealand?

In order to thoroughly explore this idea, the following supporting sub-questions were developed to be used as a guideline for the research design. Through detailed investigation of each sub-question, an in-depth exploration of the central research question can be made, thus leading to the desired outcome – the identification of a best practice model that can be implemented in small-scale event management to generate improved value and stronger growth.

- To what extent does an agreed theoretical framework exist to guide the management of large-scale special events?
- To what extent has this framework been tested across a variety of settings?
- What specific challenges are evident in small-scale events that are not present in large-scale events?
- What lessons can managers of small events learn from the experience of big events?

In order to gather necessary data around this topic, the researcher became personally involved in a small-scale and local event, from initial planning stages to eventual event operation. The overall intention was for the researcher to act as a participant observer for, by becoming part of the event management team, he was better able to understand the team's actions and decisions, and to compare their actual approach to management with the theoretical practises identified in the literature. The results that emerged from this process provide a foundation for a comparison of actual small-scale event management practises with theoretically optimal practises derived from previous observation of large scale events.

1.3 Book Outline

The book is structured around three main content sections. In the first section the literature is reviewed, in the second section the methodology and research design is illustrated, and in the last section the findings are discussed and recommendations proposed. This structure has been chosen to make it easier to communicate content to the reader and to distinguish between the intent of each of the sections.

The first section literature review is essential for a clear understanding of the topic. It contains a variety of definitions taken from a range of differing literatures, and investigates those topics that have been variously held to be important indicators to the successful management of events. The review concludes by identifying a potentially useful model by which to assess event management effectiveness.

The second section of the book introduces the research methodology and design process used, on the commonly understood principle that the approach to the conduct of research is critically important in determining the results obtained and recommendations offered. Thus, the paradigmatic approach used in this research is explained and justified in the light of the main implications involved, and the process used to gather data fully described.

The third section of this book presents the outcomes of the research, reached through application of researcher analysis and interpretation to draw conclusions and make recommendations that include:

- Critical analysis of the approaches and decisions made by event staff, and evaluation of their effectiveness in the light of theoretical recommendations.
- Comparison of similarities and differences between the planning and execution of small and mega events.
- Presentation of a best practice framework for smaller, local events.

At the end of this research, the existing body of knowledge about best practice in large-scale event management has been tested through application to a small-scale local event in New

Zealand. The implications and lessons learned during the test extend the existing knowledge about small-scale local events, and the knowledge thus gained can be used to improve the performance of such events around the world.

2. Literature review

2.1 Prologue

Davies and Brown (2000) write that *"festivals and events are special times in people's lives, they give us the opportunity to go outside normal experiences for a cultural, social or leisure experience"* (p. 169). The public use of the word *'event'* does not necessarily concur with the scientific use of it (Loos, Hermes, & Thomas, 2008). The literature available is mostly not concerned about defining the word event prior to undertaking research in the field, which leads to communication gaps and misunderstandings.

To prevent common misunderstandings this literature review defines, discusses and structures the comparatively young industry of event management. It starts with the origin of the word *'event'* and the industry of event management, followed by the importance, the influencing factors and the skills of people within the industry. The last part of the literature review is devoted to a framework of best practices in event management. The outcome of the literature review is a base to work from throughout the book and beyond.

2.2 Event Management Defined

2.2.1 Events

The word *'event'* is derived from the Latin word *'eventus'* which means *"outcome, result. success."* Further research into the etymology of the word *'eventus'* on ("Event," 2009) describes the line of descent as the following: Eventus is derived from the Latin word eventum (occurrence, event, issue), which is derived from the Latin word evenire (come out, it happens, it turns out), which is derived from the Latin word venire (to come, go for sale).

This line of descent gives the conclusion that originally an event is an occurrence, something that happens. The first mentioned definition in the English speaking world originates from Robert Jani in 1955. Jani said that *"a special event is that which is different from a normal day of living"* (Jani, 1955, in Goldblatt, 2005, p. 6). Since then, written sources have not settled on a single generally accepted definition of events.

Getz (1997) defines events as *"temporary occurrences, either planned or unplanned"* (p. 4). To describe the difference between unplanned and planned events, the word event is preceded by the word *'special'*, to indicate a human element; therefore a special event is a *"one-time or infrequently occurring event outside a normal program"* (Getz, 1997, p. 4). Due to the human element of planning and managing, events have been growing rapidly and have become bigger and bigger.

For the purpose of the book and with regards to the event industry we will use the term special event to describe a planned, temporary occurrence that is outside the daily routine of people. To shorten the spelling, the term special event will be abbreviated to event.

2.2.2 Event Management

Management has its roots in the Latin word *'manidiare'*, which is derived from the Latin word *'manus'* (hand, fist, team) ("Management," 2009). The word *'management'* is used to describe the activity of organizing a group of people to achieve a desired outcome. In Henri Fayol's *Administration industrielle et generale* from 1916 he describes the five principle roles of management in business as planning, organizing, leading, co-ordinate and controlling (usually within a company or a department of the company) to work together (Olum, 2004).

Combining the words *'event'* and *'management'* the growing profession of event management emerges. Since Jani's comment in 1955 events have evolved from a "different from a normal day of living" (Jani, 1955, in Goldblatt, 2005) to professionally managed high profile events such as the Olympic Games and the FIFA Soccer World Cup.

For determined people who want to work in the sector a lot of challenges and opportunities are awaiting. With the fast growth of the event industry, there has been growing demand for greater collaboration between academia and event practitioners to increase the uptake of research findings (Getz, 2000; Neale, 2000) and to develop professionals that will be able to handle the challenges of the industry in the future (Arcodia & Barker, 2003; Mc Cabe, 2001).

Today there are studies on Congress Management, Corporate Events, Management of fairs and exhibitions, Trade Fair Marketing and Development, Strategic Communication, Event projects Budgeting, Financing and Controlling of Events. The growth in the field of event management is continuing in all areas, such as academic, credential, knowledge transfer and qualifications, however according to Goldblatt (2000) *"the rapid growth of the event management profession has produced a climate that is confusing, lacking in credibility and compared to other professions, and perhaps detrimental to its future long term health."* (p. 2)

2.2.3 Types of Events

To handle the confusion Arcodia & Barker (2003) have categorised events into three main groups which are business events, cultural events and sporting events. Business events include conferences and trade fairs, while cultural events include festivals and exhibitions. The sporting games are the last group and include the Olympic Games, soccer world cups, car races and many other sporting events. These groupings seem to be appropriate as they encompass all sorts of events and allow the researcher to give the audience a more specific, categorised overview of events.

2.3 The History and Background of Event Management

Event management is, compared to other fields of social sciences, a relatively new field. Academic research into the field of event management has not started until about 15 years ago. In 1994 Getz & Wick's examined global trends in event management and summarized the situation of the event industry with the following quote: *"Festival and Event practitioners belong to a new and rapidly growing career field. As with other emerging quasi-professions, the managers, marketers and co-ordinators occupying full-time positions have organized professional associations and are seeking certification. Those wishing to enter the field look to the associations, and increasingly to formal educational institutions, to provide appropriate certificates which will hopefully ensure access to the better jobs. As well, numerous volunteers are seeking recognition for their efforts and skills. Consequently, the situation is somewhat unclear and constantly evolving"* (p. 103).

Regardless of the description of event management to be used, it is obvious that *"planned events have significantly changed in volume, size, scope, and quality since Jani issued this definition (in 1954)"* (Goldblatt, 2000, p. 3). Getz & Wicks concluded their research by saying that *"there are clear technical skills for event management, but less convincingly can there be said to exist theories of event management"* (1994, p. 108).

In 1996, Perry, Foley & Rumpf conducted research at the Australian Events Conference in Canberra and identified ten knowledge areas and attributes required to be successful in the event industry: project management, budgeting, time management, relating to media, business planning, human resource management, marketing, contingency management, obtaining sponsorship and networking. Those skills were categorized in the five domains legal/finance, management, public relations/marketing, economic/analytical and ethical/contextual, to create a knowledge base for future event managers. These skills seem to be a contentious issue, as vision, leadership, adaptability and high organizational skills were named by the same managers as the essential attributes to be successful in the field (Perry et al., 1996).

Subsequent to the research above, Harris & Jago (1999) suggested that the following knowledge should also be transferred in event management training:

- *History and meanings of festivals, celebrations, rituals and other events*
- *Historical evolution, types of events*
- *Trends in demand and supply*
- *Motivations and benefits sought from events*
- *Roles and impacts of events in society, the economy, environment and culture*
- *Who is producing events and why?*
- *Program concepts and styles*
- *Event settings*
- *Operations unique to events*
- *Management unique to events*
- *Marketing unique to events* (Harris & Jago, 1999, p. 46)

While a common knowledge base could not be supported at the research, a high level of education of the professionals within the event industry has been identified with over 60% having a degree and 25% having post grad qualifications. Despite these seemingly impressive figures, *"only 12% had qualifications in the event field"* (Royal & Jago, 1998, p. 224).

Comparing today's course outlines for event managers at Unitec New Zealand, BIZ, Germany, and other universities, a common base of knowledge included in the subjects of event management cannot be determined. It becomes remarkable truth that obviously no generally accepted common base has evolved out of the suggestions of the various researches that has been conducted over the last 15 years.

Harris & Jago (1999) surveyed Australian Universities and discovered another obstacle. Most Universities do not create an event program, but rather add single courses or electives to already existing programs. This method enhances the understanding of the event field within students of other fields, but it does not support event practitioners in the field and it does not create enough research on the topic of event management.

One of the reasons is that not all researchers agree on the necessity of long term event management training as appealed for by Harris & Jago (1999), they do prefer short courses where knowledge is mediated in seminars and applied straight away. Goldblatt (1997, 2000) goes a step further when he writes that the measure of professional knowledge and capability cannot be represented by a university degree. Arcodia & Barker's (2003) suggestion to employ highly trained and experienced individuals to educate the future event managers has to overcome the obstacle that there is no common base to compare with the knowledge of these professionals.

Despite the variety of literature about event management, Erber (2002) and Holzbauer (2003) both emphasize that the core elements of event management in the past often only entail organizational and controlling measures as part of the event execution. Loos (2008) objects this assessment and highlights that the definition would exclude the integrative tasks of management with decision making options. He describes event management as *"the coordination of all the tasks and activities necessary for the execution of an event regarding its strategy, planning, implementation, and control, based on the principles of event marketing and the methods of project management"* (Loos et al., 2008, p. 54).

In view of the current state of affairs, the conclusion of Getz & Wicks from 1994, as mentioned at the beginning of this section, has not lost its actuality and validity. Harris, Jago Allen & Huyskens (2000) are sharing the same opinion and think *"to determine the current state of research within the events field is not necessarily an easy task. Even though the area is still largely 'virgin territory' from a research perspective there is still, both globally and in an Australian context, a not insubstantial number of reports/articles/book etc dealing with events"* (p. 24)

Nelson (2004) researched the *"Sociological Theories of Career Choice: A Study of Workers in the Special Events Industry"* for her PhD and discovered several traits and qualities that people in the industry have in common. Surprisingly, most of the interviewed practitioners did not plan to work in the event industry but were into it introduced by chance. Despite their dissimilarity in education all of the practitioners share one common trait: they are open to new ideas.

Nelson's key findings were:

- Even in the real world business arena, post career entry, event professionals tend to relay stories about continuing to make business decisions on a visceral level.
- People who stay in the industry feel lucky to work on something that they are passionate about every day
- Event professionals suffer from particular career challenges, such as long working hours, reduced employee benefits - but they are only minor considerations regarding career entry
- Event professionals feel connection with "making dreams come true" – building a dream for somebody else
- *"Predominant decision-making factors used when choosing a career in the special events overwhelmingly supports Social Identity Theory. The highest rated factors included interesting work, opportunity for self-expression, and freedom of action. Therefore, the tie between occupation and identity (personal values) would seem to be apparent among special event workers, and supports Turner's view of a role-person merger where the role is deeply merged with the person and socialisation in that role affects personality formation"* (Turner, 1978 in Nelson, 2004, p. 46)

Nelson (2004) summarized the key findings as practitioners in the field feel *"extremely lucky to be able to work at something every day that they love"* (p. 50)
The client/provider relationship was identified as the main challenge within in the industry. With a strong sense of helping others, a passion for the industry and a lot of pride in excellence in their work, event managers overcome those obstacles and create value (Nelson, 2004).

While event managers have a lot of pride in the excellence of their work they were not enthusiastic to engage in theoretical research about strategies further improving the excellence within the entire event industry. There are several assumptions about the reasons behind it:

- Most of the people in the industry did not plan to work on events and therefore they did not engage in theoretical event studies
- The event industry offers only reduced employee benefits and hardly any benefit are expected from engaging into research
- Theoretical knowledge does not reflect the level of expertise within the event industry and event managers concentrate on gaining practical knowledge
- The long working hours within the event industry prevents people from doing additional work
- The event field is wide spread and some literature would only be relevant to a small portion of the industry

The multiple views on event management and the different perceptions of the people working and researching within the event industry has prevented the industry to come up with globally accepted standards for events.

Furthermore, the discrepancy between the aims of the different stakeholders has prevented the introduction of standardised processes and hindered the introduction of a widely accepted event management information system until today. Partial solutions have been introduced but their propagation has been limited due to these same factors.

Still, special events have evolved to the point where their number, scale and variety, combined with their associated economic, social and cultural impacts, demand attention from researchers (Harris et al., 2000, p. 22).

2.3.1 An Overview

The growth within the event industry shows that people have been successful in consistently creating bigger and better events, however the lack of widely accepted standardised processes in the industry leaves the question of how this is achieved in dispute.

The event industry has to face the same global actualities other industries have to deal with as well. Getz (2000b) investigated how the global actualities in 2000 influenced the event industry and what perspectives were arising. His findings are presented in the following table:

Table 1: Disciplinary Perspectives on Events

Environmental Perspective	(related disciplines: natural and environmental sciences; physical geography; environmental design and psychology) • trends: new event themes (e.g., whale festival in BC) • greening of events (e.g., Olympics) • ecologically sustainable tourism and sustainable events (criteria) • festival/event venues
Community Perspective	(related disciplines/fields: anthropology; sociology; community planning) • events as leisure and social opportunities; celebration • cross-cultural studies • social problems at events • social/cultural impacts on the community; host-guest interactions • cause-related events
Economic Perspective	(economics; finance; tourism; economic development • place marketing; image • tourism; seasons; animation • economic impacts • costs and benefits; distribution of
Event Programming	(recreation and sport; arts and entertainment) • education through events • retailing and exhibiting effectiveness
Law	• impact of the regulatory environment; risk management; incorporation or charitable status; protection of name, logo, designs, etc.
Management Perspective	(business, public administration, and not-for-profit) • organisational management (marketing; human resources; finance; controls and evaluation; organisation and co-ordination; • hospitality management (events as service encounters; quality assurance) • tourism destination management (competitiveness; image enhancement; marketing)
Psychological Perspective	(psychology; social-psychology) • motivation to attend and benefits sought from events; links to satisfaction • gender, culture, demographic and age factors affecting demand
Political Perspective	(political science) • political goals • propaganda through events and to sell events

(Getz, 2000b, p. 14)

To get a better understanding of the realities and how the perspectives would change the event industry he went on and investigated how the forces in 2000 influenced the implementation of the perspectives and the focus of people within the event industry. To better understand the forces he pioneered in coming up with research implications to deal with the upcoming topics professionally. The following table depicts the actualities and the resulting research implications.

Table 2: Major Forces Affecting Event Management

FORCES	RESEARCH IMPLICATIONS
DEMOGRAPHICS • Ageing population • baby-boomers the dominant segment • immigration a major force	• what do seniors want? • echo-boomers? • unknown implications of changing population mix • what marketing messages work best?
ECONOMICS • more money, less time • continued growth in tourism; many short trips • expanding meetings/expos sector • more women working and making decisions • highly competitive destinations • less government subsidy • more for-profit events	• what are consumers willing to pay? • how can value for time be maximised? • how exactly do events contribute to destination competitiveness? to profitability? • what are the impacts of increasing dependence on corporate sponsors?
TECHNOLOGY • the Internet as a major force • global media coverage of events • technologically sophisticated consumers • numerous competitors for leisure time	• how to maximise the benefits of the web • more media events - what is their value? • what technology do consumers expect and use (e.g., ticketing, booking, information searching) • getting the next generation away from their computers
CULTURE AND VALUES • increasingly multicultural societies • environmental values • experience orientation • special interest groups proliferate	• how to use events as a unifying force? • ways to make events greener, safer, more experiential for consumers • evaluating the many perspectives on event worth

(Getz, 2000b, p. 16)

With the current trends and the challenges arising in the event industry there is a high demand for creative managers who add value to the events while matching the ideas of the client with those of the organisation (Bilton & Laery, 2002). The globalisation and the ease of travel nowadays, combined with the developments in technology, it is becoming more important to continuously educate students and event managers. The Meeting Professionals International (MPI), one of the leading industry associations, has introduced an *'Excellence Strategy'* in 2003 which classifies competencies for professionals in the meeting and event field. One critical part is the identification of key knowledge, expertise and capability. In 2003 the Global Paragon was awarded for the demonstration of value through measuring meetings by their ROI (return on investment)(Nichols, 2003). One of the jury members described the value added by the winner the following way: *"Across the board, what set the winners apart was that they set goals for themselves, then structured them in such a way that they could measure them and understand exactly where they stood in terms of their successes and failures afterwards"* (Zielinski in Nichols, 2003, p. 1).

Getz (2000b) analysed the global trends and challenges and how they affect the event industry. To deal with the upcoming trends he suggested research topics to focus on. The table underneath depicts his findings and recommendations.

Table 3: Trends and Research Implications

TRENDS	RESEARCH IMPLICATIONS
CONTINUED GROWTH • more events • larger, with greater impact • diversity in theme, style, organisation, goals	• what is the saturation level? • do events have a predictable life-cycle ? • how to gain sustainable competitive advantage? • fostering innovation in programming
STRATEGIC EVENT DEVELOPMENT • for tourism and economic development • for urban renewal • for cultural and social goals • for private-sector marketing	• • is goal displacement a problem? • what events work best to realise tourism and economic goals?
SPECIAL-PURPOSE EVENT VENUES • convention and exposition centres • festival places • recreation and sport complexes	• are they all viable? • what are the professional skills needed in programming facilities through events?
SPONSORSHIP • responsible for event growth and success • variable by time and place	• • how to achieve long-term partnerships? • what is the risk of dependence on sponsors?
ACCOUNTABILITY • all stakeholders want measurement of results and impacts	• developing standardised methods and measures • accounting for all costs and benefits & the distribution of each
CONTROVERSY AND PROTEST • events attracting more critical attention • protests as special events	• what is a sustainable event? • how are protest events planned? • forecasting the impacts of events from multiple perspectives
LEGAL MATTERS • protection of name, logos, designs, etc. • risk management	• predicting and managing risks to owners, staff, volunteers, customers, the environment and community
PROFESSSONALISM • event management educational programs are on the rise, globally • professional associations are mostly organised by type of event	• what are the core event management concepts, methods and skills? • how • can associations be brought together?
PRIVATE SECTOR INITIATIVES • more events produced for profit • professional event-related firms (marketing, sponsorship, programming) • more specialist suppliers to events	• what are the best business opportunities? • can certification or professional standards be applied?

(Getz, 2000b, p. 17)

It is unquestionable that events have become a significant part of our lives, and there are several trends that lead to the supposition that the event industry, if managed correctly, has prospects of further expansion. Goldblatt (2000) predicts that with the growing age of the world's population there will be a significant increase in celebrations. The requirements for all events will increase with the innovation of technology and the desire for *'high-touch experiences'*. His predictions from 2000 for the year 2010 have become partly truth and therefore his predictions for the years to follow are worth serious consideration.

Table 4: Trends in Event Management

Year	Trend	Trigger Event/Early Warning	Response
2005	Environmental	Energy costs escalate	Use of alternative energy/power sources such as methane gas and wind to power event technical systems
2005	Technological	E-commerce achieves full penetration	Shift to on-line registration/ticket sales and tracking for many events
2005	Human Resource	Generation X and Y desire shorter work week/job sharing	Re-define role and scope of full and part-time event management positions
2010	Environmental	State, Provincial, and Federal environmental regulations impact event industry	Green event certification program through non-governmental organisations (NGO's) develop voluntary standards
2010	Technological	Internet2 provides wide band real time event opportunities	Hybridisation between live in-person events and on-line live (virtual) events improves yield management and guest interaction
2010	Human Resource	Females dominate event management executive level	Shift in organisations from traditional hierarchical systems to collaborative structures; increased job sharing, flexible time bands, on-site or nearby day care, paternity leave
2015	Technological	Complete systems integration	Events and technology achieve harmonious relationship with 24 hour, seven day per week event opportunities for guests who desire to forecast, attend, and review their participation in an event
2015	Human Resource	Increased number of deaths due to aging of North American baby boomers	Funereal events increase in frequency among human life cycle event category, purpose built facilities such as 'Life Celebration Centres' replace traditional funeral homes, alternative rituals are introduced to reflect immigration trends in US and creativity of baby boomers and their children (i.e. pyrotechnic displays containing ashes of deceased as well as friends, family)
2020	Environmental	Water scarcity crisis	Developed countries conserve water and develop improved recycling and purification systems for events
2020	Technological	Interplanetary broadcasting	Guests of planet earth and guests of other planets conduct interplanetary event using advanced communications technology
2020	Human Resource	Human capital needs are replaced by technological capital advances	Event staff become highly specialised as more and more functions are performed electronically
2025	Environmental	Major advances in medicine, agriculture, and other sciences	Incident and risk exposure is significantly reduced at events due to precise forecasting and intervention measures. Health of event staff will improve due to early diagnosis resulting in alteration of lifestyles, medications, and medical procedures. This will result in a much wider age span for event staff including octogenarians as well as young adults.
2025	Technological	Full robotic capability	Events are totally automated enabling event professionals to significantly expand the number of simultaneous events being produced using fewer human staff
2025	Human Resource	Life long learning systems developed	Human beings will be capable of significant intellectual development throughout their lives (now averaging over 100 years) and therefore the qualified workforce for events will improve and increase as well as age.

(Goldblatt, 2000, p. 8)

One major obstacle to prepare the event industry for the upcoming challenges is the existence of lots of different stakeholders for every event and each brings their own individual views and considerations. As a consequence, *"the design of event management processes, as well as the systematic development of supportive information systems have not occurred"* (Loos et al., 2008, p. 39). Harris, Jago Allen and Huyskens (2000) summarize the dilemma of event management:

"Practitioners and Associations, as would be expected, are primarily interested in research associated with generating funds, namely, sponsorship, as well as the needs of different consumer segments. Government is more interested in economic and risk factors as well as the ability to compare different events. Academics tend to be more interested in macro issues such as strategy, value of the industry, destination image and urban revival" (p. 27).

To trial the maturity of event management as a profession the Capability Maturity Model (CMM) gives valuable insights. The Capability Maturity Model depicts the processes and procedures rather than the artistic outcome o an event and therefore it shows the maturity of the system rather than the outcome of the system (Bamberger, 1997). While the outcome of an event might be positive, it might not be possible to apply the same processes and procedures to other events. As a result, the Capability Maturity Model depicts the immaturity of the event management profession with the lack of formalization, standardization, accountability, and continuous improvement practices (Silvers, 2003).

Silvers (2003) went one step further and compared the levels of the CMM with Bloom's Taxonomy, a 1956 developed classification of levels of intellectual behaviour with regards to learning. She concluded that "the hierarchy of maturity for performing organizations and individuals is practically parallel" (Silvers, 2003). The following illustration shows the comparisons:

Figure 5: The CMM and Bloom's Taxonomy Intellectual Maturity

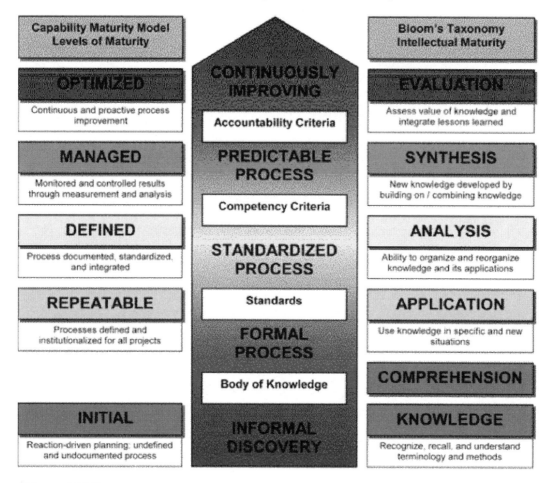

(Silvers, 2003)

Today, more training opportunities are increasing the percentage of people who have a degree relevant to their event occupation. Without a generally accepted body of knowledge the variety of studies in the field of event management is enormous and support the arguments of McCabe (2001) and Neale (2000), who find it necessary to create a body of knowledge; to ensure professionalism and to educate managers in the field to handle current and future challenges within the industry, as depicted above.

This goes in hand with Goldblatt's three essential elements of a profession. As illustrated at the end of the last section they are a common body of knowledge, established and maintained standards and a code of conduct (Goldblatt, 1996 in Royal & Jago, 1998). At this stage we can recapitulate that the literature does not support the existence of the first two elements.

This is consistent with the research of Arcodia & Reid (2002), who identified a need to further develop and educate event professionals to ensure professionalism. In addition to education, Arcodia & Barker (2003) suggest that improved collaboration between academics and practitioners is needed. Academics and practitioners are falling short of their potentials because they are not working in close partnership, and the future success of the event field will depend greatly on its ability to realise its own potential.

The next section will go one step further and give a picture of best practices in event management.

2.3.2 Best practices in Event Management

The history of best practices in event management begins in 1992, when a Canadian consortium introduced a set of *'occupational competency standards'* with consideration towards administration, risk management, management skills, marketing, interpersonal skills and HRM (Harris & Jago, 1999). In 1996 Perry, Foley and Rumpf (1996) conducted the first research in Australia (and the first for the southern hemisphere). They attempted to identify event organisers' training and education requirements and came up with the following key knowledge areas:

- Legal / financial
- Management
- Public relations / marketing
- Economic / analytical
- Ethical / contextual

This research assumed that a good knowledge base about the best practices in the above fields would lead to a successful career in the field. Other research disproved the findings.

Getz and Wicks (1994) confirmed that *"management theory and skills are essential, but their application... requires adaptation similar to that required for recreation management. And because there is so much variety among event types and settings, it can be argued that only generic concepts can be taught, with experience providing the detail"* (p. 108). Their research identified energy and ambition as the key success factors within the event industry.

On top of energy and ambition, creativity has been identified by various sources as key to creating exceptional events. Creativity is the part that makes an event unique and distinguishes it from previous ones organized by the same manager, company or organization. A lot of research has mentioned the importance of creativity while planning events (Allen et al., 2008; Bilton & Laery, 2002; Fabling & Grimes, 2007; Getz & Wicks, 1994; Silvers et al., 2006) but none of them attempted to create a framework for best practices in the area. It is reasonable to assume that artistic expression is hard to measure and therefore difficult to put into a framework, but it is nevertheless a worthwhile venture.

Slivers et al. (2006) continue in the same vein when they write that the combination of *"creativity, strategic thinking, continuous improvement, ethics and integration are the values that must permeate all decisions throughout event management regarding every element, phase, and process"* (p. 192), and only have to be adjusted to the needs of different cultural conditions.

One of the obstacles that research into best practices in event management has to face is that funding is mostly given for the investigation of the social, economic and cultural effects of events. Sponsors, especially governments, are more likely to invest in continuous events when the research shows that the event has a positive impact on the community. Consequently, *"less research has been focused on special events operational management"* (Hede, Jago, & Deery, 2002, p. 322). At the same time, governments are influencing the execution of events by devising laws and acts in order to limit the negative influences of events. With the lack of international or even national standards for the evaluation of events, the event environment is becoming more complex and regulated, as every town, city, community, country, and continent has different laws in place, and it is hard for professionals to maintain a synopsis.

It can be argued that event managers are artists and that it is their conscious decision to continue their dynamic and creative way of doing things (Meusburger, Funke, & Wunder, 2009) rather than supporting the creation of *"reliable, disciplined and consistent systems"* (Colline, 2001, in Silvers et al., 2006, p. 192) which could transform the current *'people-dependent'* system into a *'system dependent'* system (Gerber, 1995, in Silvers et al., 2006, p. 193).

The confusion the current situation is producing results in the lack of respect and value for the industry along with limitations to the funding and support by officials (Goldblatt, 2000). It can be expected that the creation of an effective quality assurance system would improve the quality of the individuals within the industry and would allow for the creation of standard terminology to be used for events and festivals (Arcodia & Robb, 2000). It would clearly change the focus of the research from economic and marketing concentrations to standards and frameworks. The industry could ameliorate from an immature occupation to a well-established, highly-respected profession through the creation of a conceptual framework to recap present knowledge and best practises for event professionals.

Every city and town around the world has the potential to host events. For locations who want to tap into the future growth of the event industry and who want to be continuously successful in doing so, it is imperative to handle their assets properly. Melbourne is an excellent example for a destination that successfully implemented its events strategy early on and created value on a national basis while managing its potential with care and determination. The first business plan of Tourism Victoria in 1993 (*Strategic business plan*, 1993) identified the priority of developing and attracting special events and subsequently repeated the importance in the next business plan in 1997 (*Strategic business plan 1997 - 2001*, 1997).

The city tapped its ability to host successful special events and was host of the World Police and Fire Games, the Formula One Grand Prix, the Australian Open, the Melbourne Cup and uncountable smaller events (Royal & Jago, 1998).The strategic plan to attract events has not only led to the hosting of those events, it has also attracted a large number of professionals to live and work in the city. The City of Melbourne introduced networking opportunities to tap the knowledge of its citizens and to find ways to attract more visitors to the city. The combined knowledge and political backup has led to a vibrant event environment that is thriving.

Melbourne's economy has gained largely from the professional management of its event environment. The public and the private sector are working together for the benefits of all stakeholders. The city is one of only a few examples around the world where best practices for the attraction and hosting of events have been established with all the benefits coming with it.

With the Formula 1 Grand Prix and the Australian Open tennis on its calendar, the city hosts two of the major events of the Southern Hemisphere, ensuring that the image of the city is continuously displayed worldwide. Following the success of Melbourne, cities all over Australia have attempted to compete for world class events, and event management *"has emerged to become a key sector of the Australian tourism industry"* (Arcodia & Barker, 2003, p. 2). The drawback of the momentary fast growth of the event industry is that it was not organic, but rather erratic and *"has produced a climate that is confusing, lacking in credibility as compared to other professions, and perhaps detrimental to its future long term health"* (Goldblatt, 2000, p. 2). Nevertheless, the economic benefits of hosting events make them worth taking a chance on, even though globalisation has made the staging of global events more competitive than ever. An example of this would be the bid for the 2016 Olympic Games, won by Rio de Janeiro.

Baum and Lockstone (2007) have noted that *"interest in all aspects of the politics, financing, planning, management and operation of mega sporting events has been highlighted both by success stories and ongoing problems associated with Olympic Games, Football World Cups and other similar events. There is a growing literature that addresses these and related matters through both case history and comparative analyses"* (p. 29). There is also an increase literature about the impacts of events on cities, communities and countries (Hiller, 1995; Jones, 2001; Kim & Petrick, 2005; Lee, Lee, & Lee, 2005). The Soccer World Cup in South Korea, in particular, was researched a lot, but the research provided *"little that is definitive to guide policy makers and politicians along a path of certainty in their decision making in this area"* (Baum & Lockstone, 2007, p. 30). This statement indicates that there is a lack of decision making guidance for policy makers and politicians when deciding on the realization and support of an event. To support the decision makers and to get political support from them, it can be argued that a framework of best practices for event management could be of value. The framework would guide the event team and make the outcome of any event more predictable.

In the current economic climate in particular, money for events is limited and clients are reducing funding to events and demanding more securities for the events they are planning with regards to the outcome for the companies. Until the early 2000's research focused on economic evaluations after the event (Clarke, 2004), since was necessary to find indicators to measure performance against before research could, in the next step, find indicators to use to evaluate the event prior to its execution.

In 2008, Loos, Hermes and Thomas highlighted the importance of evaluations during the planning of events to achieve sustainability. They voiced for the introduction of risk management and controlling within all stages of the event; a clear indicator that there is no framework at the moment.

Goldblatt (2000) asks for a pilot project to be introduced for a three year period to test the viability of different processes and reach a framework of best practices. This study will not fulfil his request to the full extent; however, the next section will attempt to come up with a framework of best practices based on Goldblatt's recommendations in his book: *Best Practices in Modern Event Management (1997)* and test the framework against current practices in New Zealand.

So far we have concluded that, at this stage, that there is no agreed theoretical framework to guide the management of large-scale special events and consequently a framework has not been tested until today. To answer the third and fourth sub-questions it is necessary to create a framework of best practices of event management. Given the scarcity of referenced journal articles on this subject, the literature foundations for this venture are necessarily focused on books written about the topic, and here it is clearly possible to note the distinction between those written by practitioners and those written by academics. Practitioners tend to focus on the design, planning and coordination of the event rather than the theories that underpin its management – for example, Tum, Norton and Wright (2006) have a clear emphasis on the importance of time, risk, and supply chain management, while Goldblatt (1997) focuses on the design and creation of an overall event environment.

2.3.3 A Matrix of Best Practices

An extensive literature review has identified various options to create a framework. The most appropriate option was found in Goldblatt's (1997) *Special Events: Best practices in Modern Event Management* where Goldblatt identified four essential pillars of event management which he defined as time, finance, technology and human resources. These pillars can be combined with the slightly modified five principle roles of management in business as identified in Henri Fayol's *Administration industrielle et generale as planning, organizing, leading co-ordinating and controlling (Olum, 2004).* For the purpose of the research the five management processes of research, design, plan, co-ordinate and evaluate will be used to create a 5x4 matrix (Arcodia & Robb, 2000; Bartholomew, 2002; Hinch & Higham, 2001; Tum et al., 2006).

Combining the management processes and the pillars the following matrix emerges:

Table 6: 5x4 Matrix of Best Practices in Event Management

	Research	Design	Planning	Coordination	Evaluation
Time					
Finance					
Technology					
Human Resources					

The combination of Goldblatt's (1997) pillars and the five management processes created a 5x4 matrix that will was used to build a framework of best practices in event management. The framework was enriched and improved through an extensive literature review about best practices in various elements of events. The result is a synopsis of the available knowledge of best practices in event management presented in a framework of best practices for the first time ever.

As everything that is created for the first time, the framework has its limitations as there is no international consensus on best practices and it can only be used as a foundation to start with. Other researchers are invited to expand, improve and comment on it. With the large variety of events it is understood that the framework cannot be too narrow, as it would limit the creativity of practitioners, neither can it be too broad, as the value of the framework would be limited. The framework attempts to link depth and breadth of the topic.

Before the framework can be filled with the synopsis of the available literature on best practices, it is essential to define the four pillars and five management processes that build the structure of the 5x4matrix to ensure a common base of understanding.

Research

Most special events start with an idea. Someone wants to create an event and has a vague idea what it could or should be like. Research is the first step to make this idea come true, as it is the search for knowledge about the matter at hand and the starting point for all progress. With a deeper understanding of the past and the current possibilities we can influence and change the future. With a better understanding of the customers and clients needs and wants and the feasibility of these needs and wants, the event manager has a higher chance of achieving the imagined outcome for the event. Research will reduce the risk of not achieving the goals of an event.

The value of research into expectations, needs and desires has been highlighted by various sources, such as PR professionals and marketing experts. Governments go through extensive feasibility analysis before spending any money on products and events. After a first broad research into the idea and its feasibility a project plan is created to give the decision makers a broad idea about the feasibility of an event and a base for supplementary research. It identifies target groups, sets measurable goals (strategic, operative and economic), identifies marketing strategies and stets the structure of the event planning team.

Design

After researching the *'hard'* fact about an event, design focuses on the creative aspects of an event. Design has to be approached differently than research, as it is not static or predictable. Design is the creative process that makes the event different from other events that have gone before; it gives the event its uniqueness and therefore requires a lot of inspiration and ideas coming from various sources. It is very important for the event manager to support and highlight the importance of ideas coming in from their team. At this stage brainstorming is a very important tool for bringing ideas together to create an outstanding event.

It is important to be clear about the core reason for the event, and make this the centre point around which the discussion revolves. It is also important to create a suitable environment for staff to work creatively, as different individuals often require different approaches to help stimulate ideas. A great deal of experience is required to facilitate successful design meetings with staff members. Once these creative meetings have been held it is important to give structure to the ideas and to compare them with the actual goals and requirements of the event.

An approach to needs assessment, according to Goldblatt (1997, p. 43):

Why?   >What is the compelling reason for the event?
            >Why must this event be held?

Who?   >Who will benefit from the event?
            >Who will the client want to attend?

When?   >When will the event be held?
            >Is the date and time flexible or subject to change?

Where?   >What is the best destination, location and venue?

What?   >What elements and resources are required to satisfy the needs identified
              above?

Next to the needs the feasibility of every item has to be checked with regards to finance, human resources and political influences. Depending on the event at hand this can be quite different to other events before as you might rely on volunteer work, expertise, or special people. How to determine the strengths and weaknesses of the people involved is quite an important task as well. They need to function together efficiently.

With the lack of a framework for event management politics has taken over the responsibility to set minimum standards for event professionals. In some nations those standards are quite strict; in other nations the standards are loose and bendable. It is important to approach the right people to get the permits and decisions needed to go ahead with the project.

Planning

The planning process is the stage where the quality of the work of the two previous stages becomes palpable. In this stage the requirements from the previous stages will be concretized and customized to the client's wishes. With good in depth research and an appropriate design the planning can focus on getting the pieces together. The planning stage can be disastrous because in unveils the mistakes from the previous stages and forces the event manager to rethink his research and design.

Depending on the input from the previous stages and the requirements for the event the team will be put together. Team building lessons from project management can be integrated when it comes to big events. Especially mega events will divide the event in smaller projects to be realized by teams. After installing the teams focus can be given to the conceptual options for the event.

There are two main phases involved in this stage: Time & Space

Time refers to the time the event manager has until the event is scheduled to happen. In most cases the date of the event is set and the event manager has to get the event together by then, still, there are times when the event manager can influence the timings to better fit the occasion, weather, schedule, ... In both occasions the timing influences the costs of getting an event together.

Time also refers to the time the event manager has available. When he is working on other events that might be influenced negatively due to time issues the event manager has to evaluate if it is worth taking on the job. Considering how much time the team has put into the research and design of the event has to be balanced with the professional quality the event manager wants to display.

According to Goldblatt (1997) **space** has two dimensions: The space where the event will be held and the space between critical decisions for the event. Especially the second dimension is closely linked to the timings for the event.

With regards to the venue for the event there are several considerations that should be made before booking the location, such as parking, decoration, atmosphere and others. Atmosphere can be of immense importance as it saves a lot of time when the location does not need a lot of set up time. Loos, Hermes and Thomas (2008) suggest a three-dimensional presentation of the prospected venues to get a better understanding of the aspired result for the event manager and for the client. Goldblatt advises to *"use a critical friend – a person whose expertise about the particular event is known to you – to review your plan and specifically search for gaps in your logical thinking"* (Goldblatt, 1997, p. 55) . Appendix 1 shows a checklist of considerations when inspecting a possible location.

Coordination

This stage is the part where the actual event happens. It is the ultimate test of the quality of work done in the previous stages combined with the nature of unpredictability that comes with every event. All the preparations and the planning of the staff will be tested and emphasis will be on short-term problem solving to keep a smooth running of the event.

The coordination stage starts with the dress rehearsal as the last test of the pre event set up and planning. Often the dress rehearsal gives the event manager the opportunity to test his set up and it will identify several challenges that have not been thought of.

There is one main issue the event manager has to consider before the event and stick to it throughout the event: the staffing. Especially big events will not allow the event manager to overview every detail himself. He needs to dichotomise tasks and delegate responsibilities to the most appropriate individuals and trust in his choice.

Evaluation is the task that can be of enormous value for future events. It is a dynamic process that changes with the event and the stakeholders involved. Some events might just require a short debrief while others require an in-depth analysis with a sophisticated outlook of future influencing factors. A good evaluation always starts with feedback of the attendees, since a survey is mostly used form of analysis. Another good way of getting an idea of the satisfaction of guests is the usage of an observer, a person who observes an event with regards to a checklist and offers additional comments.

A relatively new, but highly efficient way of evaluating an event is the pre- and post event survey. It shows the discrepancies between the expectations before the event with the actual delivering of the event. It helps to close gaps that might have gone unnoticed otherwise.
Goldblatt (1997) also advices to seek feedback during the event and stay close to the guests. This will enable the event manager to get an immediate feeling for the satisfaction of the guests and might enable the event manager to influence the outcome of the event.

2.3.4 The Four Pillar Approach

After defining the management processes for the 5x4 matrix of best practices, this section defines the four pillars time, finance, technology and human resources and analyses the best practices within each of the pillars. To achieve the goal of a comprehensive summary a large spectrum of literature has been analysed and compared with regards to best practices. At the end of this section the reader should have a profound overview about the current literature of best practices in event management.

To simplify the understanding, the best practices have been categorized within the 5x4 matrix as introduced in the last section.

Table 7: The Four Pillar Approach

FIGURE 1-2
The Four Pillar Approach:
A Foundation for Success

EVENT MANAGEMENT

Time   Finance   Technology   Human Resources

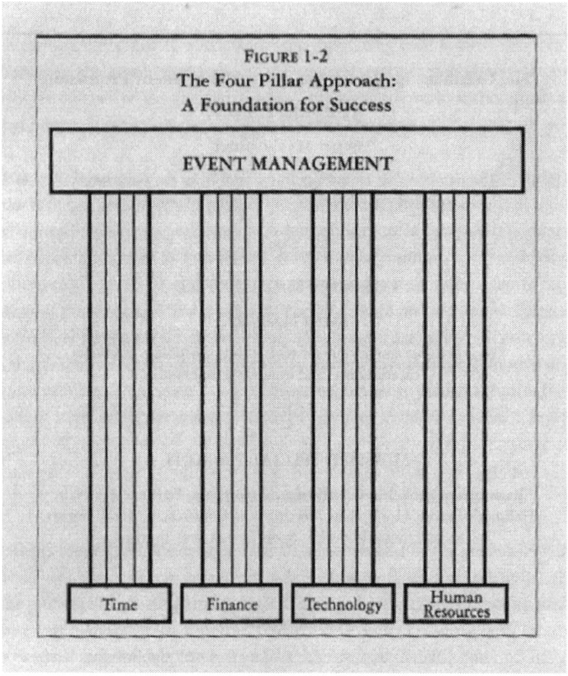

(Goldblatt, 1997, p. 12)

Time is the most pressing issues when organizing events. Without a good timing events could never run as smooth as most of them do.

The first pillar of event management is *'time'* with the two categories value of time and critical path.

Value of time

Time is one of the most scare resources of humankind, once invested it is gone. The field of event management is very time consuming and therefore time is a very important consideration. The event manager needs to assess the value of his time and charge it to the event. For example The EDGE®, an Auckland based convention centre, has an event number for every event and staff members are asked to add the event number on their time sheets. Knowing about time is important because it helps analysing the actual costs of an event and it gives staff a limit on the time needed for the planning of an event.

Goldblatt (1997) has identified several best practices for event time management. Next to the importance of knowing the worth of time an event manager needs to limit time wasting activities and get a database of contacts to refer to instantly.

The worth of time allows charging every event with the amount of hours put in and it enables the event manager to limit the time put into time wasting activities. The following suggestions were made:

- Budget the time depending on personal priorities (work, meetings, family,...)
- Determine the worth of your time (place small signs next to the phone and computer)
- Prepare a daily to do list (move unfinished activities to the next day)
- Determine the importance of meetings (cancel them if they are not important)
- Assess if you are the right person to receive phone calls
- Handle e-mails only once
- Organize a written agenda for every business meeting (Good to prepare for the meetings and o get the key points)
- Create a database including a calendar and detailed information about meeting partners to check on them before every meeting.
- Entrust capable assistants with tasks whenever possible.

Critical path is a term taken over from project management. The critical path connects the tasks included in an event and shows how these tasks are related and how long the project will take if all dependent tasks could be undertaken after each other. It then depicts the earliest and latest possible starting time for each task with regards to the dependencies and shows when activities will have to start without influencing the earliest possible finish time.

Finance is the issue that has to be kept in mind. There are several reasons why events are happening, but nearly none of them has an unlimited budget to spend without any income.

The second pillar is *'finance'* with the aspects overall costs of business, sponsorship and marketing & promotion.

Overall costs of business

There are several ways to organize an event but in every case there has to be an organization or a company behind who the event manager works for. In most cases the event manager works for his own company and signs a contract with a client, company or institution to organize an event. In some cases the event manager works for the organization and realizes the events for the company. Goldblatt (1997) identifies five best practices for the financial success of the company:

- *Set realistic short- and long –term financial goals*
- *Seek professional counsel*
- *Identify and use efficient technology*
- *Systematically review financial health*
- *Control overhead costs* (p. 16)

The above identified five best practices are necessary to continuously create great events. They are the backbone of a successful company and ensure that the employees continuously get their money and can focus at the task at hand. Experiencing financial problems is connected with a high level of stress and can lead to the deterioration of a business (Gorgievski, Bakker, Schaufeli, van der Veen, & Giesen, 2009).

Sponsorship can be a very important for the success of an event. All major events around the world have sponsors, companies who support the event in exchange for public exposure. Sponsorship makes an event financially feasible and ensures the quality standards of events. In the research process it requires a lot of time to analyse the needs and requirements of the event and find appropriate sponsors. Therefore it is most common to have sponsors for big events where the work involved justifies the estimated benefits of a sponsor. In the research part the following checklist has to be considered:

- *Is the event feasible without a sponsor?*
- *Is there enough backup for a sponsor?*
- *Does sponsorship fit to the event?*
- *Does sponsorship fit to the organization (spirit, legal, ethical)?* (Goldblatt, 1997, p. 251)

If the outcome of the research indicates the necessity of a sponsor the second step would be to identify appropriate sponsors and work with them towards the realization of the event. Applied to the five processes of event management this means:

Research:
- Examine the extend of required sponsorship
- Research sponsor activities at other events
- Analyse the local market to find prospectus sponsors
- Contact advertising and PR companies to identify possible interest

Design:
- Conduct a focus group to scout attitudes toward the event.
- Customize the event to reflect sponsor's needs and objectives.

Planning:
- Qualify the sponsors through profound research
- Apply sponsor's action pan
- Reconsider sponsor's changes and additions
- Implement the changes and update sponsor

Coordination

- Ensure visibility of sponsor
- Evaluation

After the event it is essential to meet with sponsor to evaluate the success of the event and assess further projects (Goldblatt, 1997).

Marketing & Promotion

The modern age has made the marketing and promotion for an event even harder, as people are exposed to an ever increasing number of publicity through an increasing mix of channels. A study conducted by Gitelson and Kerstetter (Gitelson & Kerstetter, 2000 in Smith, 2008) emphasizes the potential complexity of promotions for events. The findings indicated that local people would use the newspaper as source of information while nonlocal people would refer to local friends and relatives for information. For both groups previous experience was the main source of information.

Surprisingly Smith (2008) concluded that for most promotions past experience was more important than effectiveness of the channels. Research was only conducted past the event with the limited amount of information available from ticketing agents and event manager's observations.

"Promotional channels such as radio, television, newspapers, magazines, posters and banners, were all significant in raising awareness of the event, but not highly rated as the most important source of information. Internet was not highly used despite all the events having a dedicated website and the three ticketed events having online booking available through their ticketing agent. Media sources tended to be supplementary information sources" (Smith, 2008, p. 30)

In his conclusion he highlights the importance of understanding the information sources used by attendees and the way they make their decisions. For example, *"access to attractions by public transport and on foot is of greater importance to overseas visitors at urban destinations than access by private car"* (Thompson & Schofield, 2002, p. 41).

Ralston, Ellis, Compton & Lee (2007) emphasize the importance of word of mouth as the most trusted and most efficient way of marketing any city, agency or event. Most industries have the advantage that they can market their products in relation to other products, because people know similar products to compare them with. Events are different. Every event is unique and therefore it is hard to compare events with previous or other events. The tendency to create bigger and better events every time increases the difficulty of comparison.

Even mega events require a promotional strategy to ensure that all events and ideas connected to the event will be successful. The FIFA soccer world cup in Germany 2006 was highly successful because the organizers introduced and professionally managed large public viewing areas in nearly every German city. Media people broadcasted from the best parties around the country and enhance the atmosphere around the event. The public viewing concept was also highly profitable and inspiring.

The information mix for events has been heavily researched and the two main distinctions are free access events and ticketed events. For free events the distribution of information is highly important. Ticketed events require far more work than only providing information, they also have to deal with reservations and payment issues. These factors *"influence the structure, operation, and effectiveness of event distribution channels"* (Smith, 2008, p. 35). Goldberg (1997)has created a checklist for promotions to ensure that a high quality event will not be the best kept secret in the world:

Research

- "Identify all event elements that require promotion from the proposal through the final evaluation

Design

- Develop strategies for allocating scarce event promotion resources with efficient methods

Planning

- Identify promotion partners to share costs
- Carefully target your promotion to those market segments that will support the event

Evaluation (throughout the event)

- Measure and analyze your promotion efforts throughout the campaign to make corrections as required" (Goldblatt, 1997, p. 231)

Technology is the single most important issue when creating an event. Modern technologies allow us to communicate with people around the world, get information and do the research necessary to evaluate the chances of an event.

The third pillar is *'technology'* with the sub categories overall code of conduct, entertainment, communication, benchmarking and location.

Overall code of conduct

The Greek origin tells us that technology is the study of the craft. There are many crafts in the World and therefore technology is a broad concept, but it can be applied to the specific area of event management.

First, and most importantly, technology can be used within the event company to accelerate processes and efficiently enter data such as financial spreadsheets, customer information and latest requests. It also enables a company to charge expenses straight to an event instead of creating a large amount of overhead costs.

Goldblatt (1997) identified several best practices for event management technology that are independent of the event processes:

- Spot the technology needs within your company
- Evaluate and acquire appropriate technology

- Establish technology in collaboration with your employees
- Periodically investigate requirements for professional work and adjust new technology

Entertainment

Entertainment is a part of every event. People come to events to divert themselves from their daily life and expect amusement and attractions to get out of their routine and experience something new. Entertainment is the most common purpose of events, and recreation, that is, being active as part of the diversion, might be included in some events.

Entertainment becomes a priority during design process, as the event team has to determine how they want to achieve the goal of the client and what kind of entertainment they will provide. As there are a variety of events the resources have to be analysed first:

Research
- Investigate the history of the event and determine the size of the live audience.
- Determine the importance of entertainment and technology for the goal of the event

Design
- Consult the stakeholders to ascertain their tastes and analyse the audience with regards to education, age, cultural background, learning style, previous experience and likings and identify appropriate entertainment
- Inspect the venue to see how your entertainment could be realized and whether available onsite resources will be sufficient
- Change perspectives and imagine the event as a guest. Evaluate how the guest would experience the entertainment and if your resources are enough to bewitch every guest (Goldblatt, 1997), because *"any sufficiently advanced technology is indistinguishable from magic"* (Arthur C. Clark in Schneiderhahn, 2002, p. 1)

The process of planning the entertainment is relatively straightforward once the design has been finished. For the interested reader appendix 2 will depict how to effectively manage the entertainment after the design has been completed and give the overview of the technical terms within entertainment.

Communication

There are several recipients of communication and an effective and efficient communication strategy is essential for the success of an event.

During the research process the target audience has to be distinguished and the needs of that market segment have to be analyzed; in particular, the most common information channel used by the target audience must be determined. Smith (2008) highlights the importance of information sources for any event. Uncertainty obstructs people from going to an event and the basic event information needs to be conveniently available. A properly managed communication strategy is important for building customer loyalty and ensuring continuing success.

Virtual communities are a frequently used source of information and have great potential to reach a large group of people, but the use of these communities should be based on the traditional PR model, where an official statement is released first and people can refer to it all the time (Beaven & Laws, 2008). This ensures clarity from the beginning.

With the growth of an events company the distribution of event information is becoming more significant and manifold at the same time. One way of managing and developing relationships with potential visitors is through membership databases. For smaller companies friend groups or information from ticket agents are vital sources means of disseminating information.

Smith (2008) emphasized the importance of on-the-day information sources. He looked at the Wellington Dragon Boat Festival and discovered that about 20% of spectators learned about the event by passing by which led him to the assumption that other information sources were not used.

Shanka and Taylor (2004) conducted correspondence analysis to investigate the information sources of festival visitors. The analysis discovered that there is a discrepancy of information used between local residents and non-residents as non residents would prefer road signs and newspapers ad while locals rely on word-of mouth advertisement.

An investigation into the information sources preferred by specific age groups noted that the visitors in the 18-24 age bracket rely more on word of mouth advertisement, the 25-35 age bracket relies more on websites, and the over 55 age bracket uses the local newspaper to acquire information.

This research was carried out in Western Australia and it should be noted that the findings within the 18-24 age bracket might not be a true representation as most 18-24 year old festival visitors in Western Australia are overseas backpackers who gather together to exchange information about places and events to go (Shanka & Taylor, 2004).

Table 8: A Comparison of Findings

Table 5: Comparative Summary of Findings

Information Channel		SUPPLY Information sources distributed by event organisers	DEMAND Information sources used by event attendees	Match?	Implications for event organisers
Range of channels		Multiple channels to reach target markets	Use multiple sources of information		
Event-generated information	Print & broadcast media Visual presence in destination	Important, particularly as an awareness-raising call to action	Used but not rated as the most important	Mismatch of importance – more highly rated by organisers than attendees	Although not rated as most important by attendees, still needed to raise awareness so requires effective spending strategy
	Brochures	For complex programmes (e.g. festivals) – most important channel	For complex programmes – most important information source	Match	Need to ensure effective distribution strategy for brochures (e.g. through partnership with sponsors)
	Internet	Key to future distribution/information mix	Used as a supplementary information source. More important for tourists	Partial match - neither events nor attendees are widely using the Internet but organisers see future growth potential	Ensure that investment is matched by attendee's online use. Greatest potential for reaching non-local markets
	Direct mail/ membership databases	Very significant for those with membership databases	Important for events with membership base (e.g. festival friends)	Match	Potential for future development of membership relationships, including season ticket holders and ticketing databases
Previous Experience	Prior attendance and word of mouth	Recognised but not necessarily as part of information mix	Most important, especially when high level of repeat visitation, but needs to be supplemented by other information sources	Mismatch – more highly rated by visitors than organisers	Requires focus on service quality
Third parties	Tourism-related channels	Very limited, focus on distribution to tourists at destination	Limited use, even at destination	Match – little use	Potential for development (e.g. Visitor Information Centres), however, difficult and costly to effectively reach tourist markets at origin
	Education/work links	Distributing information through participants can reach spectators	Important when supporting friends, family & colleagues as participants	Match – at participation events	Further develop distribution through participants
By chance		Significance recognised for free events	Important for free, open access events	Match – at free events	Hard to predict visitor numbers (and operational implications) so need to supplement with other channels

(Smith, 2008, p. 34)

Benchmarking

EventsCrop WA, an organisation in Western Australia charged with developing, managing, and assessing significance of local events in Western Australia, is currently working to develop a uniform tool to objectively and systematically measure the various impacts of events. Currently each event company uses a different methodology and formula to describe the outcome of the event and therefore it is difficult for event organisers to compare apples to oranges as they attempt to benchmark their event operations and outcomes against each other's (Goldblatt, 2000).

The **location** of an event is the single most important consideration at the beginning of the preparations of an event. The wrong location can cause all kinds of trouble and adjustments and can force the event manager to react, rather than act, on the issues that have to be dealt with.

During the research process possible locations are identified and discussed. It is not until the design process that the event manager knows most of the details and can conduct a site inspection with the event in mind. In his book *Best Practices in Modern Event Management* (1997), Goldblatt dedicates more than four pages to a checklist regarding the site inspection alone. This checklist is attached in appendix 1.

A positive aspect of having a checklist is that it can be handed over to staff members in case the event manager is not available for the inspection or the location is not in the vicinity where the event manager is based. The site inspection requires imagination and insight as it is an opportunity to analyse how the needs of clients and patrons can be met.

The planning stage requires what Goldblatt calls a 'sensory audit and plan'. This plan accommodates the five senses – tactile, smell, taste, visual and auditory – to powerfully satiate the needs of the guests. It is crucial for the event manager to get the client creatively and emotionally involved in the planning of the event. Goldblatt (Goldblatt, 1997, p. 64) suggests the following steps:

- *"Use a focus group to determine the primary sensory stimuli of your guests.*
- *Identify any oversensitivity or even allergies your guests may have that could be irritated by certain sensory elements.*
- *Use a draft diagram of the event environment to identify and isolate the location of certain sensory experiences.*
- *Share the design tool with typical guests and solicit their attitudes and opinions.*
- *Audit the venue to determine the pre-existing sensory environment and what modifications you will be required to implement."*

The next step in the planning process is the decor of the event. Most events hire a professional company to take care of decoration; nevertheless, the event manager needs adjust the decor to the purpose of the event and the sensory audit. Attachment 3 offers the interested reader a checklist for decor.

After the event the location will be evaluated and possible improvements will be noted for the next event.

Human resources are the base of an event, because without people no one would come to organized events. And it is also the people behind the scene that are creating the events, event managers, technicians, sponsors, supporters, volunteers... They all contribute to make events happening.

The fourth pillar of event management is *'human resources'*; the sub-categories of human resources are management, staff, volunteers and customer relationship management (CRM).

Management

As shown at the event management section of the literature review, the term 'management' refers to the tasks of planning, organizing, leading and controlling a group of people to achieve a desired outcome. In terms of event management that outcome may vary from event to event, but the management of the event organization needs to establish clear goals for its employees, and know and pursue the competitive advantage of the company.

Competitive advantage is an advantage over competitors gained by offering consumers greater value, either by means of lower prices or by providing greater benefits and services that justify higher prices. The event environment is traditionally very competitive and prices have been lowered in recent years, but event managers are well known for their creativity and therefore most companies compete by providing greater benefits to their clients. While some companies compete in the organisation of events, other companies specialise in niches within the event industry such as the operation of incentive holiday.

One strategy to gain a competitive advantage involves the selection of criteria the clients consider when hiring an event company and evaluating the strengths and weaknesses of the event company. This step should also include the opinion and perception of current customers. The results need to be compared to competitors who are working in the same field of events to gauge the real competitive advantage of the company.   With this information at hand, the managers can come up with a differentiation strategy has the potential and the backbone to put the event company ahead of its competition.

The next step to keep the competitive advantage is the implementation of ground rules for the employees of the company to ensure the differentiation strategy is applied in the marketplace and customers can experience the talk of the management. After a few months it is necessary to review the strategy and give feedback to the employees. While this process sounds similar to the processes of an event it is different as it affects the entire company.

With consideration to the differentiation strategy, Goldblatt (1997) mentions best practices for decision making within event companies. The considerations can not only be used for the implementation of a differentiation strategy, but also for the preparations of an event:

- Attain all the information from as many perspectives as possible
- Think about all people who will be affected by the decision and how they will be affected
- Evaluate the ethical implications of the decision
- Gauge the financial changes of the decision

- Once the decision is made there are no more considerations

Another source of information on the topic of *'management'* can be event management associations. Part of their strategic agenda includes the development of mission statements. Arcodia and Reid (2002) explored the mission statements and revealed a strong tendency towards *"education promotion, networking, communication, ethical standards and professionalism"* (p. 71).

Staff

The famous American football coach Lou Holtz once said: *"It's not my job to motivate players. They bring extraordinary motivation to our program. It's my job not to de-motivate them."*

The connection between an American football team and the staff of an event company might not be clear at the first glance, but several surveys of attitudes to employment within the event and convention industry showed that there is an above average level of commitment from the people working within the industry. McCabe (2001) found that *"there was evidence of a high commitment to employment within the industry, with the career chosen in the field of convention and exhibition management seen positively as being the best possible career choice that they could have made"* (p. 498).

As mentioned above the field of event management guarantees different tasks and challenges every event. Practitioners have to deal with different customers and, as depicted in the management section, the company competes on a quality/differentiation strategy all the time. People who work for one of the big event companies generally work within an interesting and inspiring team that achieves high standards and creates new ideas to meet client expectation in the process. Event managers are forced to be creative and the best they can be. Consequently, it is of no surprise that people within the industry are exceptionally pleased by their career choice in comparison with their peer group (Mc Cabe, 2001).

Goldblatt (1997) also mentions the importance of lifelong learning, and suggests that every successful event company needs to continuously support his employees to aspire a high level of competence and strive to achieve this level. From a company view he suggests:

- Enhance continuous learning within the company and budget resources to it
- Financially and emotionally support employee learning and training
- Offer a study group towards certifications
- Build a ring of education where every employee gets a certain reading time and has to share the information with the people of his team
- Attend ad send employees to conferences and exhibitions and to collect new ideas and teach other staff members

Volunteers are the single most overlooked workers within the event industry. The fact that volunteers usually only work at mega events is partly responsible for the fact that barely any research is conducted on the subject of volunteers and their motivations.

Nowadays the success of events depends on the fulfilment of various expectations. Events *"must also embrace a plethora of other requirements..."* (Mc Donald, Allen, & O'Toole, 1999, p. 39), and for mega events the throng of volunteers are the face of the event. In most cases they are the first contact point for most visitors, spectators, media and other stakeholders. They create a first impression people for attendees of the event.

The motivation and satisfaction of volunteers at mega sport events has been somewhat researched in the past, but their economic value as been seriously overlooked (Baum & Lockstone, 2007). Volunteers not only save event organizations large amounts of money, they also create enormous value for the event.

Customer Relationship Management (CRM)

The contract to deliver an event is the first milestone an event company has to achieve, but customer relationship management starts long before the actual signing of a contract. After identifying a potential client the event manager undertakes a certain amount of research to get a better understanding of the event and the requirements of the potential client. The findings will be presented to the client. Goldblatt (1997) introduced a five step plan to effectively present pre-event research findings to a client which can be distilled into four steps:

- Determine your audience and customize the presentation to their personal communication learning style (Goldblatt, 1997, p. 36)
- Illustrate how the research has been done and the implications, opportunities and the limitations of the research
- Highlight how the event company can be essential in achieving the key strategic goals
- Invite questions and create collaboration

Once the research part has been successfully completed, the event manager will usually focus on the planning of the event rather than convincing the client. During the design process, in particular, a transformation has to take place - from a business transaction to relationship management, where the event manager works together with the client to plan the event according to the plans and imaginings of the client. This requires a good sense of the needs, wishes and desires of the client, combined with enough imagination to create an event that fulfils all requirements.

Guests are the audience and the reason why events happen. Without guests there would not be any events, event industry or event managers. Every event has a different kind of audience and the special need of the audience of the event at hand have to be taken into account. Special needs might include VIPs, people with disabilities, special nutrition requirements, etc. During the research period the likely audience has to be verified and their special needs have to be identified to successfully bid for the event.

In the design part the event manager needs to work closely with the client to decide how to meet the expectations and the special needs of the guests and how to implement the clients' ideas about the design of the event.

The planning phase will provide conclusions about the actual people attending the event and necessary alterations may have to be made. An appropriate welcome for VIP guests must be in place and well-trained personnel for the check-in have to be organized. In the co-ordination stage the event manager receives the first feedback revealing the quality of his or her planning and can react to complaints if necessary.

It is advisory to hand out feedback forms for the guests to be filled in at the end of every event to enhance the evaluation of an event and to propose alternating activities for the next event.

Ralston et al describe the outcome of a perfectly planned event with the following quote: *"When [visitors say] "I didn't know there were such beautiful and interesting places!" what they are really saying is that they did not know that they had within them such capacity for the realization of beauty and significance. They fall in love with the national parks, not for the spectacular features within them, but for the essence of them. They do not say this in self-conscious words, but they feel it"* (Ralston et al., 2007, p. 28).

Catering and other suppliers

Most event companies do not cater for events; they are more likely to organize an outside catering company for an event. Some locations might have their in house catering or pre arranged catering companies and the event manager do not need to select the caterer.

At the design part the site inspection should still include to check out the catering possibilities and specifications. Depending on the event the following requirements might be necessary:

- Full service set up with 24/7 room service
- Licence requirements
- Diversity of food selection and stylish presentation

The relationship between the event manager and the caterer/vendor should be built on trust and mutual respect and therefore it is good practice to learn about the suppliers and to know how significant your event is to them. Other best practices include:

- Determine how attractive it is for the supplier to do business with your client, e.g. is there potential for a long term relationship
- Learn about the standards and the sophistication of operations of the supplier
- Get familiarized with the payment options you have and talk to other clients of the supplier to compare their terms with yours (Goldblatt, 1997).

Further information about the best practices for the logistics for effective catered events can be found in appendix 4. Goldblatt(1997) provides a 10-point checklist for preparing catering proposals.

Table 9: Catering Checklist

Catering Proposal Checklist

1. History of the catering organization including other clients of similar size and scope they have served.

2. Letters of reference from other clients of similar size and scope.

3. Complete description of cuisine.

4. Complete description of style of service including the number of servers/bartenders that will be provided.

5. Complete description of equipment that will be provided by the caterer. Equipment may include tables, chairs, and serving utensils as well as other items. Make certain that each is described and that quantity is included.

6. Listing of additional services to be provided by the caterer such as floral, entertainment, or other special requirements.

7. Complete description of payment terms including date of guarantee, taxes, gratuities, deposits, balance payments, and percentage of overage provided by the caterer.

8. All schedule information concerning deliveries, setup, service, and removal of equipment through load-out.

9. Insurance, bonding, and other information pertinent to managing the risk of your event.

10. Any additional requirements including utilities such as water, electric power, and so on

(Goldblatt, 1997, p. 168)

2.3.5 The Synopsis of Best Practices in Event Management into a 5x4 Matrix

This section summarized the findings of the review of a large spectrum of literature about event management. The literature has been reviewed with regards to best practices in event management and the information of all relevant articles has been added to the 5x4 matrix of best practices of event management. At this stage it is the first collection of literature about best practices put into a raw framework.

This framework is envisaged to be a starting point for discussions and a basis for the evaluation of small scale events within New Zealand. It is hoped that the framework has the potential to be used in practice once it is refined and improved.

No literature proved to cover more than one or two topics as most literature focused on different components of events. A large spectrum of literature had to be scrutinized with regards to the matrix. The following table depicts the best practices that have been identified during the literature review. It is intended to give the reader a quick overview of the topics that have been identified.

The matrix does not claim to be perfect or complete. It is rather a starting point for discussions and shall invite people to contribute.

Table 10: The Framework of Best Practices in Event Management

	Research	Design	Planning	Coordination	Evaluation
Time					
Value of time					
Critical Path					
Finance					
Overall costs of business					
Sponsorship					
Promotion &					
Marketing					
Technology					
Overall code of conduct					
Entertainment					
Communication					
Benchmarking					
Location					
Human Resources					
Management					
Staff					
Volunteers					
CRM					
Catering & other					
Suppliers					

Later on in this book the framework is tested for the first time.

2.4 Shortcomings and Aspirations

Up to now the literature review has summarized the short history of event management and has introduced a 5x4 matrix of best practices in event management filled it with best practices derived from a large spectrum of literature. The matrix attempts to give the reader an overview of the existent research which proved to be a task in itself, because *"to determine the current state of research within the events field is not necessarily an easy task. Even though the area is still largely 'virgin territory' from a research perspective there is still, both globally and in an Australian context, a not insubstantial number of reports/articles/book etc dealing with events"* (Harris et al., 2000, p. 24).

The confusing structure of the existing knowledge let Getz (1998) to looked into the management processes of events. He concluded that, compared to other industries, the field of events is not assessable as the processes are just evolving and have not reached the stage of clear terms for evaluating the management practices. Even now, more than ten years later, this conclusion has not lost its validity. Goldblatt (2000) argued that the fast growth of the industry is to blame for the climate of confusion and the growth did not slow down until the financial crisis recently. Still, special events have evolved to the point where their number, scale and variety, combined with their associated economic, social and cultural impacts, demand attention from researchers (Harris et al., 2000, p. 22).

The confusing structure has led event managers to rely more on their expertise than on their training, which is the *"most dangerous and expensive form of learning"* (Graham, Goldblatt, & Delpy, 1995, p.26 in Nelson, 2004).

One possible way of handling the confusing structure is the introduction of a recognized event management body of knowledge which would fulfil one of Goldblatt's (1997) three expectations on a profession. Major constraints with the introduction of a body of knowledge have been identified by Silvers, Bowdin, O'Toole & Nelson (2006). They state that *"the lack of data, research and the recognition of common processes are major constraints to forming an event management body of knowledge"* (p. 17). Other publications concur with that statement (Getz, 1998, 2000a; W. J. O'Toole & Mikolaitis, 2002).

There are several indicators that the lack of credibility that has not been gained in the past will now effect the industry negatively and only experienced companies with a background of proven expertise will get projects, while new companies will diminish. As a result the current conditions could be a perfect time to develop a framework for international event management, to introduce measurable standards that set a path towards establishing event management as a true profession. The framework would have to be broad enough to include the large variety of event genres, but still be lean enough to work with. Such standards would enable and enhance research in the field right from the beginning and throughout the project, rather than focusing only on the output of events, as it is today.

In many industries, the introduction of a framework and accreditation systems has led to quality improvements and increasing professionalism (Royal & Jago, 1998). The current environment puts clients under monetary pressure and therefore they demand more sophistication and higher quality. Standards in the events industry are rising, but the fulfilment of those expectations is left to chance so far.

This book can be seen as a first step towards an official framework. While the last sections structured the available literature about event management in a new way, the next sections depict the possibilities and shortcomings of the 5x4 matrix when applied on a small-size event. The advantages include:

- For educators: A foundation for course composition and curriculum evolution which leads to international comparability of education and expertise (Silvers et al., 2006).
- For employers: To compare education and expertise of employees and to work with universities to equip young professionals with the skill set required in the field.
- For industry professionals: A starting point for professional progress and comparability with other event managers (Silvers et al., 2006).

3. Methodology

3.1 Philosophical Foundations of Research

It is commonly understood that the nature of the specific research question will have a significant influence over the methodological approach adopted and the data collection methods used in the research field work. Thus, though the literature review and the subsequent creation of a draft framework of best practice will inevitably set the path for the researcher, and it is important that the researcher remains focused on investigating the topics raised through the framework, it is equally important to ensure that this does not result in a limited creativity and a possibility of being blind to new ideas (Collis & Hussey,

2003). In order to address this possibility, this section begins by considering the options open to the researcher in terms of research paradigm adopted, and continues on to describe the methods used to assemble the data necessary for subsequent analysis.

3.1.1 Qualitative research

Qualitative research, as a component of the phenomenological paradigm, aims to *"describe certain aspects of phenomena, with a view to explaining the subject of study"* (Cormack, 1991, p. 29). Qualitative research uses small samples and tries to identify the empirical world of the subject investigated (Duffy, 1987). In contrast to quantitative research, qualitative research accepts that the *"act of investigating reality has an effect on that reality"* (Collis & Hussey, 2003, p. 53), therefore the interrelationship between investigator and the investigated subject is not only part of the research, but also intentional. Qualitative research focuses on the causes behind outcomes rather than the measurement of outcomes, and uses the researcher as a key point within the research. The researcher is not afraid of influencing the results, but in contrast will consciously bring his own particular knowledge and experience.

The importance of data collection method selection has been described by a range of researchers (Bell, 1969; Cassell, Bishop, Symon, Johnson, & Buehring, 2009; DeWalt & DeWalt, 2002; Haug & Teune, 2008; Kawulich, 2005; Marshall & Rossman, 1989; Merriam, 1998; Participant observation in logistics research: Experiences from an RFID implementation study," 2007; Šindlárová, 1999; Turner, 2009), and ethnography has been used as an umbrella term for qualitative methods of data collection within anthropological and sociological studies. The word ethnography is derived from the Greek words *'ethos'* = folk, people and the word *'graphein'* = writing and the methodology is used to describe research into human societies. As a result, this methodological approach is able to *"encompass interpersonal, social and cultural context"* (Hara, 1995, p. 353) and is capable of including individual dimensions that reveal a deeper insight into human behaviour and its implications. In this respect, Kawulich (2005) includes the techniques of participant observation and interview as components of ethnography, taking the view that humans are best understood by gathering as much information as possible while they are within their native environment.

3.1.2 Participant observation

One very common approach is direct, first-hand observation, which includes the technique of participant observation. This method has long been a hallmark in anthropology and sociology, and has now spread to other fields of social science such as education, logistics and geography. Participant observation has been a commonly used *"tool to collect information about people, processes, and cultures in qualitative research"* (Kawulich, 2005, p. 1), and requires that the researcher immerses into a community and uses the five senses to interpret and portray existing situations and events. The method has been defined by Marshall & Rossman (1989) as *"the systematic description of events, behaviours, and artefacts in the social setting chosen for study"* (p. 79), and requires the researcher to gain admittance and access to the population of interest, in order to observe and take notes about everything that is noteworthy.

Bell (1969) was one of the earlier thinkers in the field of participant observation, and tried to formalize this method of data collection by providing a framework to depict the various roles a researcher could take with regards to the procedures and ethical considerations that were relevant to the situation being investigated. Bell categorized social systems, such as institutions and organizations, by their ease of access and their 'openness', and combined these data with a researcher choice of working overtly or covertly to generate four possible combinations:

- Overt entry into an open system
- Overt entry into a closed system
- Covert entry into an open system
- Covert entry into a closed system

For Bell, these distinctions were important, as *"overt entry into an open system involves publicity, into a closed system sponsorship; covert entry into an open system involves stealth, into a closed system guile"* (Bell, 1969, p. 417).

Since Bell's research in 1969, the importance of participant research as a source of information has been repeatedly highlighted (Haug & Teune, 2008; Participant observation in logistics research: Experiences from an RFID implementation study," 2007; Tope, Chamberlain, Crowley, & Hodson, 2005). For example, in a discussion held at the Harvard Business School in 1983, the importance of observation in education was discussed and most participants admitted that the data they used in the classrooms were derived from personal experience in organizations – these educators confessed that they trust their own practical experience more than scientific journals, for experimental and survey research seemed to lack an understanding of the organizational realities (Schein, 1987, in Poggenpoel, Myburgh, & Van Der Linde, 2001). Similarly, the article *Tools for Creating and Measuring Value* ("Tools for Creating and Measuring Value," 2007) examined the richness of the information gained through this method to conclude that it would be difficult to gather as many significant details with any other method; while Tope et al (2005) examined the yield in ethnographic research to conclude that participant research extracts more detailed information of behaviours and group dynamics than any other method.

DeMunck & Sobo (1998) depict several further benefits of using participant observation, noting that it gives access to otherwise hidden cultural dynamics and allows for detailed observations of behaviour, intention and situations of participants. Participant observation also allows the researcher to get an understanding of the processes and dynamics that exist at a deeper level than the more obvious ones - DeWalt and DeWalt (DeWalt and DeWalt, 2002 in Kawulich, 2005) identify the advanced quality of data collection and interpretation as a clearly positive aspect of the method, noting that this can be used as a base to develop and further refine the research question; and Darling (1998) notes that the method is effective in enhancing the understanding of the circumstances of social life and its meaning to participants in those social situations:

"Both field practice and service-learning programs report common benefits that include personal growth and greater awareness and appreciation of diversity and other aspects of social life, development of practical and interpersonal skills, career awareness and academic focus and critical thinking skills, including the ability to apply academic concepts to an understanding of real world situations" (Darling, 1998, pp. 341, 342).

The success of this method does however also depend on the researchers' *"capabilities to cultivate their relationship within the unit and the maintenance of their professional approach and detachment"* (Šindlárová, 1999, p. 33), for an important aspect that limits the reliability of participant observation is the level of access to information. As mentioned above, the researcher has a choice as to how deep he chooses to become involved in the study group, and this highlights the important issue of identification and participation as a difficult choice, involving as it does the researcher being required to also perform within the group (Kolaja, 1956). Participants' feelings of being observed can themselves alternate their behaviour, notwithstanding the behaviour alterations that can occur when the researcher chooses to get fully involved into the researched situation. As a result, the observations made are always reflective of the researcher's individual interests and sources of information, and may neglect some aspects of situational culture.

DeWalt & DeWalt (DeWalt & DeWalt, 2002, in Kawulich, 2005) argue that this level of access and participation can vary according to differing characteristics of the relationship between people and settings, and conclude that the researcher is a biased human who needs to be aware of the affects of *"gender, sexuality, ethnicity, class, and theoretical approach"* (DeWalt & DeWalt, 2002, in Kawulich, 2005, p. 5) on the analysis and interpretation of his observations. Thus, the collection of data and the analysis of data constantly influence each other, putting high expectations on the individual to adjust the methodology to the field of research.

In summary, participant observation is a qualitative research method in which the researcher aims to see the world through the eyes of the subject (Riley, Newby, & Leal-Almeraz, 2006), in order to get a better idea about the work that they do, to share their experiences, and to observe the skills they need to develop to perform their task. It is inductive research, as the researcher tries to identify and understand what he is observing, rather than the deductive approach of attempting to validate a preconceived idea through hypobook testing. This inductive approach also recognises the pragmatic consideration that life changes constantly, and that the researcher therefore must participate in the life of the researched person in order to observe these changes and their outcomes.

3.1.3 Semi-structured interviews

Šindlárová (1999) writes that participant observation is usually a very time-consuming process and is therefore often combined with other research methods such as interviews. While participant observation is usually conducted by a researcher getting involved with an event, interviews can be used as complimentary form of research to get a better understanding of the concepts the people have about their work and *"the complex discursive activities through which respondents produce meaning"* (Hollstein & Gubrium, 1995, p.80 in Hiller & DiLuzio, 2004, p. 6) .

For the purpose of this research, semi structured interviews were conducted. Compared to formalized, structured interviews with limited questions, semi structured interviews are flexible and allow researchers to add and alternate questions within a pre-prepared framework. Lindlof & Taylor (2002) advice the "grouping of topics and questions that the interviewer can ask in different ways for different participants" (p. 195). This advice has been employed for the interviews of this research.

The literature on interviewing focuses on improving the yield of data collection from participants and encourages the researcher to be trustworthy and attentive to the thoughts, opinions and perspectives of the interviewee (Hiller & DiLuzio, 2004). *"In-depth interviewing is distinguished as a method that allows the researcher to explore the deeper structure of ideas presented by the participants. Two primary objectives of in-depth interviewing are exploration and verification"* (Johnson, 2002 in Stylianou, 2008, p. 242). In recent years, the traditional model of what is meant by an interview has been transformed and adopted to constructivism, an approach which highlights the mutuality of the interview process as a *"meaning making experience"* (Hiller & DiLuzio, 2004, p. 2) that creates knowledge through collaboration. This would lead to the conclusion that the individuality of the researcher influences the way the data is collected and interpreted and, consequently, this method of data collection would experience a drop in validity.

In this respect, Kolaja (1956) compared interviewing with participant observation to suggest that, in both cases, the researcher was acting, playing a part in order to extract the maximum value of information from the interviewee. However, the main differentiating characteristic of interviewing, compared to participant observation, was that the interviewer gets told about an event indirectly, after the actual event has occurred, and is therefore receiving a version of reality that the interviewee has processed and possibly elaborated upon. Thus, the selection of interviewees becomes important - Hiller and DiLuzio (2004) argue that the interview offers an opportunity to discuss and reflect on various topics with persons who have a certain amount of knowledge of the relevant field, but that certain traits in certain people may predispose participants to make this more or less likely to be an active and participative process. It is an undeniable fact that not all interviews are created equal.

3.1.4 Attendee surveys

However, just as determining the strengths and weaknesses of a person can only be done through comparison with other people, the strengths and the weaknesses of qualitative research can only be discussed by comparing this research method with the quantitative alternative.

Quantitative research, as a component of the positivist paradigm, is an *"objective, formal, systematic process"* (Carr, 1994, p. 716) which uses numerical data in order to gauge phenomena. Quantitative research is concerned with the causes and effects of relationships, and is undertaken by a researcher who takes on the role of an observer of an *"independent and pre-existing reality"* (Collis & Hussey, 2003, p. 52). This form of research builds upon existing knowledge and tries to explain enunciated hypotheses by using large samples as representative of a larger population. The researcher is believed to remain distant, and isolated from the research process, and to use their objective views to explain the causes of phenomena with little regard to their own individual state.

Surveys are generally used to get responses from a small part of a community to be used as representative of the entire community. As opposed to qualitative research methods, surveys do not need an interaction between researcher and researched person, therefore one advantage of a survey is represented by the efficiency of gathering a large number of responses in a short time. The standardisation of the survey instrument limits possible errors, and ensures that only relevant questions will be asked, while results can be interpreted with due regard to the potential for replicating them with alternative members of the same or a similar community (Borrego, Douglas, & Amelink, 2009).

However, there are disadvantages. Survey-based research may not encompass the emotions and the perceptions of people at the moment when they fill out the survey, for the answers they give may be influenced by the situation and may not reflect the general attitude of respondents (Hiller & DiLuzio, 2004).

In addition, individual characteristics, such as level of honesty and source of motivation, can significantly influences the responses received – for example, the typical motivation to reply to a survey might also influence the outcome of the survey, as the opinions of people who choose to reply may be materially different to the opinions of those who do not.

3.1.5 Mixed method approaches

Merriam (1998) raises questions about the concerns a researcher should have about his involvement and influence in the situation being researched, and names the situation a *"schizophrenic activity"* (p. 103) because the researcher needs to ask himself how he accounts for the effects of his own participation when evaluating the data. When the researcher may need to get fully involved in the action to completely understand the activity, an essential conflict arises – a fully involved researcher may lack objectivity but get access to all relevant information, whereas a researcher acting as a detached observer might be as objective as possible, but lack the in-depth experience necessary to fully comprehend the results of research.

With these considerations in mind it is understandable that, for the research at hand, several data collection methods have been chosen in an effort to achieve the best possible insights while being objective enough to describe the happenings in a manner that will offer reasonably high validity to inform other similar research projects. Kelle (2006) states that this type of mixed-method research is a methodology in social science that is widely spread despite ongoing *'paradigm wars'*. The sequential use of qualitative then quantitative approaches to research is well accepted within the social sciences research community, with qualitative methods initially used to identify major topics through interviews and observations; and to create theoretical frameworks and hypotheses that can then be tested with quantitative research methods. Quantitative methods are consequently used to test the frameworks and hypobooke with a larger sample, in order to more effectively describe social phenomena.

Though the specific research question should be the ultimate raison d'être for the choice of method (Borrego et al., 2009; Poggenpoel et al., 2001), the use of two parallel approaches increases the transferability of principles derived from qualitative research with small sample sizes into quantitative research with larger samples. While the qualitative research has the potential to reveal local insights, the quantitative methods can be used to test the meanings and relevance of the insights. In the current research described in this book, much of the data collection was based on qualitative methods that are subject to individual interpretation, and overall objectivity might not therefore be demonstrable (Kelle, 2006). Acknowledging therefore that the qualitative benefits of high validity and powerful insights into a particular situation come with the drawback of low reliability, it becomes doubly important to select the appropriate research procedures, the appropriate sample, and the most effective interpretation of results. In the following section, this process begins with the identification of a suitable event on which to base the investigation.

3.2 Event Selection

The first step in selecting an event that would be appropriate to use as an investigative framework for this research was to identify those events that were to take place in the Auckland region at a time that was coincident with the temporary residence visa and already established study responsibilities of the researcher (an international student without rights of permanent residence in New Zealand). This in itself led to a review of what events were to take place in Auckland in November 2009, on the basis that planning for these events was likely to occupy most of calendar year 2009.

To get a comprehensive overview of all events that would take place in Auckland several sources were contacted. First of all, lecturers who are teaching event management or related subjects were asked. Secondly, the book *Corporate Events Guide* was a useful source of contacts within the event industry throughout New Zealand, and Auckland especially. Other sources were people at The Edge®, event managers known to the author, events companies within Auckland and the tourism Auckland website.

After this step, the list with events that would take place in Auckland was enormous and so was there variety. The spectrum was between large corporate events such as the ballet and the opera to small dinner and cocktail parties. The researcher made a list of the features and the accessibility of each event that promised to be of value with regards to the research.

Necessary features of the event selected for study had been incorporated into the research question as *"a small-scale local event in New Zealand"* that would allow the researcher to test a framework of best practice, to investigate the type of small event challenges that are not present in large-scale events, and to assess what management skills and behaviours are particularly important in small scale event management. Bearing these characteristics in mind, five events were left as potential candidates, and selection of the final event was undertaken under the guidance of three further evaluative criteria:

- Ease of access in relation to Bell's (1969) categorisation of social systems. This is important for the researcher, as it enables him to obtain data in a form and depth sufficient to address the central research question.
- Extent to which the event was community based and reflected typical small scale New Zealand events.
- Proximity to the researcher's residence and place of study, in order that extensive participation could be undertaken without compromising the researcher's other study commitments.

Following this process, it was possible to identify two events that had been originated by institutions that were willing to offer a good level of access to the researcher, and to allow him to gain more in-depth data than the remaining three options. Both of these events were annually recurring, but while one event had a very high level of repeating content, the other much more closely reflected the type of event managed by New Zealand event managers, and this was therefore the event finally selected.

As mentioned in an earlier section, small-scale events are conventionally subdivided into the three categories of business events, cultural events and sporting events. The event studied in this research was a cultural event, an exhibition of work prepared throughout the year by a number of different artists with limited show experience. This exhibition was organised by a large institution, to support these artists in their desire to show their work to the public and, as is common in New Zealand, was organised by a fairly small committee of people with different interests and areas of expertise – in the case of the event finally selected, major representation was secured from the marketing department of the sponsoring institution, representatives of the exhibiting artists, and a number of support people such as venue designers and IT specialists. It is not uncommon for events in New Zealand to include such a range of people, and to therefore need to secure agreement and collaboration from several stakeholders before any planning can begin.

The timeline of the event, between initial planning and eventual operation, was approximately 6 months, and the event has had moderate significance for the people attending and for the local community. It commenced with a major opening function on a

Wednesday evening, and remained open to the public for a further three days after the opening. It was themed around the showcase of creativity, and displayed the artwork generated by the creative members during their last year of residence at the institution. It was mounted on behalf of a target audience that could be divided into three segments:

- Segment 1: Design sector industry representatives, potential employers, media
- Segment 2: Family and friends of the exhibitors
- Segment 3: Individuals who aspire to future participation as exhibitors

Based on previous years' statistics, the anticipated attendance was around 3000 people, though data on past attendees and their demographics was largely unavailable. This event ultimately proved to be a good choice, as it allowed the researcher to gain a great deal of in-depth data from analysis of various perspectives of the event. The methods used to gather that data are discussed in the following section.

3.3 Data Collection Methods

Lichterman (Lichtermann, 2002 in Haug & Teune, 2008) distinguishes between two approaches to research design and data collection : a deductive *'theory-based'* model which seeks to function within an established theoretical framework, and an inductive *'field driven'* model which bases itself on *terra incognita.* The research described in this book takes a theory based approach, presenting a potential framework of theory and testing that framework in the field of event management. The sections below describe the process of field testing.

3.3.1 Interviews

Interviews are a commonly used method of data collection within the field of ethnography, and can manifest in several ways from casual small talk to extended formal interviews. The basis used for the present research was that of semi-structured interviews, designed to allow a directed discussion of the topic of interest to elicit the interviewee's ideas and opinions (Cheney, Christensen, Zorn, & Ganesh, 2004). Semi-structured interviews were conducted at the beginning of the planning process with the overall event manager, two supporting event co-ordinators, and an experienced event manager who had no direct connection with this particular event. Because past research indicates that people are not always aware of their own individual strengths and weaknesses (Rath & Conchie, 2009), this cross-section of opinion was selected in order to secure multiple strands of opinion.

The guidelines for these pre-event interviews were based on elements that had emerged from the literature review as desirable elements of best practice, and the researcher aimed to get the required level of information from the interviewee, even if it were necessary to return to topics in which the necessary information was not readily given. Most questions had been pre-arranged beforehand and can be reviewed in appendix five, but these were supplemented by the addition of impulsive questions included when appropriate and deemed necessary to get more information on a specific topic. Due to the level of interaction during interviews, each occasion evolved differently, with the initially planned 30 minutes of pre-event interviews and 15 minutes of post-event interviews being exceeded in almost every case.

It had initially been planned to carry out post-event interviews with the same respondents, using the same guidelines, in order to check individual perceptions of how things had actually turned out when compared to how it was planned they should turn out. As such, the post-event interviews were more concerned with the personal perception of the interviewees with regards to their work at the event, compared to their anticipated work at the event. However, due to staff changes that had taken place during the lead-up to the event, only two such post-event interviews took place. All interviews were audio recorded on tape and transcribed for later analysis.

3.3.2 Participant observation

The researcher's personal participation in the event management process allowed him to be fully involved in the planning of this event, and to be able to fully understand the steps and actions undertaken by the event managers, the process of making decisions, and the skills necessary to ensure effective event management. In this respect, the researcher was initially able to select from four levels of involvement as proposed by Gold (1958):

- Complete participant
- Participant as observer (member of the group)
- Observer as participant (not a member of the group)
- Complete observer

In this case the researcher was involved in the planning of the event from the outset through to the event post-mortem evaluation, and it can therefore be claimed that a complete participation would best describe the situation. This particular observation was conducted according to the three basic stages suggested by Kawulich (2005), and included as Appendix 6 to this book, in order to absorb the subtle factors, such as nonverbal communication and physical clues, that occur during interactions:

- Watching the physical environment
- Recording the activities and interactions that occur
- Observing the conversation

The process of information gathering during the preparation for this event followed the above stages. Before each meeting, the researcher met with the event co-ordinator to discuss the topics for the meeting. Thus, while observation at the first meeting was primarily concerned with the physical environment to get a better understanding of the setting, subsequent meetings were used to gain a better understanding of the content of conversations and the subtle factors that lay behind them.

All activities and interactions at each of the meetings were recorded as the meeting took place, and a journal diary technique (Ross, Rideout, & Carson, 1994) was used to compile both descriptive and analytical observations of each step of the event management process. Each step along the way was subsequently analysed in depth and compared with previously identified theory, though some of the these comparisons were less straightforward than others - some steps taken in the small-scale event were not present in theory, and at small events the event manager is required to take responsibility for some tasks that the mega event manager would ordinarily delegate to others.

3.3.3 Attendee surveys

The idea of data triangulation was introduced into research by Denzin (Denzin, 1978 in Borrego et al., 2009) to describe the collection of data through the use of different and complementary methods and data sources to get a better understanding of the topic at hand. In this instance, a random sample of 10% of event attendees was asked to complete a tick-box survey that measured their degree of satisfaction with event organisation and management. These processes were designed to generate a deeper insight into the world of the event manager, and to focus on the comparison between the practical event and the theoretical framework.

Surveys are an important and frequently used research method that resides within the quantitative paradigm, and are widespread in both political polling and social sciences. In this particular case, the survey contained six different questions, four of which were closed with fixed alternative answers, and two of which were left open in an attempt to gain more detailed knowledge. The survey was completed by a request for respondent contact details and an invitation to enter a prize draw. The nature of questions may be summarised as:

- How did you find out about this event?
- What is the main reason you have attended?
- What is your level of satisfaction with event content i.e. exhibits and performances

- What is your level of satisfaction with ...
  - Availability of parking
  - Formal opening ceremony
  - Friendliness of staff
  - Overall organization of the event
- What additional features would be good to add to the event?
- Any further comments?

In this study, the aim was a response rate of 10% of all attendees with the assumption that this would be adequate to provide a representative body of data. The survey was presented to attendees through a self-administration model via public-access computers set up at the main and the main back entrance of the building where the exhibition was held. Large signs announcing the possibility of winning $50 Westfield vouchers were put up to attract people to participate in the survey.

3.4 Research Ethics Considerations

A principal consideration in any research study is the need to conduct the research in an ethical way, by letting the involved people know that they are being researched and what the purpose of the research is. This of course does not apply in some cases of participant observation, as there are occasions when covert observations might be necessary, but this approach to data collection is seldom used and was not used on this occasion.

This research was conducted by the researcher adopting the role of "participant as observer", and this is considered to be the most ethically defensible of the four possible stances mentioned earlier. As Kawulich (2005, p.7) has observed *"the researcher's observation activities are known to the group being studied, yet the emphasis for the researcher is on collecting data, rather than participating in the activity being observed"* (Kawulich, 2005, p. 7).

Nevertheless, there are still some important ethical considerations to take into account. First of all, though he attempted to limit his participation to a process of offering additional contributions to the decision process, the researcher was part of the group organizing the event and was able to bring in advice and considerations. He became involved, during the planning process, in several aspects of the marketing of the event, attempting to take over tasks that were not familiar to other people and would not have been feasible without his involvement; and he also became involve on a front-line basis in the delivery of the event itself. This level of involvement allowed the researcher to obtain in-depth insights into the quality and thoroughness of the planning process beforehand, and to additionally observe the decision making behaviours of the event manager as the event unfolded on the day.

The research project required all participants to give their consent and their participation was totally voluntary. Personal information about all of the interviewees and the details of the interviews are held to be strictly confidential, with data gathered in the interviews being secured on a personal password-protected computer. Only the supervisors and the researcher have access to these data, and anonymity of participants with regards to their comments and attitudes will be preserved. All interview files will be destroyed in three years time. In addition, it is imperative to keep the integrity and anonymity of the participants in the final version of the research. This includes the identification of the individuals and the institution that has been researched, to a degree that even the people within the relevant community will not recognize the identity of participants.

3.5 Limitations of the research

While writing this book the researcher had to create a framework of best practices of event management to answer the overall research question. While this was an interesting task, it had to be done within a limited time period and it cannot be assumed that all of the literature has been reviewed and all best practices are included. Additionally, this was the first time the framework has been tested and several potential improvements to the framework have been detected during this process – with no alternative framework in place to compare with, it is essential to supplement the ideas presented here with supplementary feedback from researchers and small-scale local event managers working with the framework. This could improve the framework substantially, but will be significantly dependent on an essential impairment that has hindered the development of the discipline to date – the difficulty in getting event practitioners to contribute to the theoretical literature.

4. Findings

The event that provided a case study setting for this research was an exhibition presented as a joint venture between several departments of a design and visual art school. Each department was required to organise a specific section of the exhibition, depending on its students' expertise and, though these departments worked in a highly sovereign way, the overall planning responsibility for the event was held by a broadly representative event management committee.

This committee consisted of one member from of each of the departments involved, and several members taken from the institution's marketing department – the marketing account manager who is responsible for the overall marketing of the departments concerned was a driving force for this committee, in the role of event co-ordinator. Other key members were the event manager whose full time role is related to the operational management of institutions' events held throughout the year, the IT service manager who is responsible for the online presence of the institution, the graphic designers who are employed by the marketing department of the institution, and the sponsorship co-ordinator who had a specific interest in the merchandise associated with the event.

As mentioned in the earlier methodology section, three different ways of gathering data were used in this project – (before and after) interviews, participant observation, and an attendee satisfaction survey. For the ease of presenting relevant information, this findings section is split according to the research methods used. Firstly, the findings of the interviews are presented, followed by the researcher's experience of participant observation, and finally the results of the attendee survey.

4.1 Interviews

The results of a series of semi-structured interviews are presented to give the reader a comprehensive insight into the processes and practices intended for use, and actually used, in the design and implementation of this event. The question outline used to guide these interviews was structured around the three main themes of event strategy, event manager skills, and personal experience with the management of past events, and aimed to guide the discussion through the five identified stages of the event management process – research, design, planning, co-ordination, and evaluation. Though it was initially proposed to interview only the event manager (now referred to as EM), one event co-ordinator (EC1), and an external event management professional unconnected with this particular event (EP), an additional event co-ordinator (EC2) was included in the process when it was discovered that the first choice co-ordinator would be leaving the management team part way through the process, due to a happy personal circumstance!

4.1.1 The research stage

The professional view of this stage, according to EP, is that a great deal of research needs to be done prior to events, as most of these have no history and are happening for the first time. EP's company has a marketing strategy that it uses to keep track of potential clients and to educate the market with regards to business events for, as EP noted, some did not know that there was such a thing as a business events industry. Thus, after an initial meeting with the client, event requirements are assessed with a specific focus on the proposed outcome of the event, where possible taking account of past experiences with previous versions of the event - *"we can ask questions about what worked and what didn't work."*

The research element of the subject event does seem to have been rather different, with EM immediately admitting that *"we don't research too much... I wonder if we have more potential there. I wonder if we should put more effort into that."* EM observed that the original version of the event involved only one department, but two other departments subsequently thought about becoming involved as they liked the concept and the potential for exposure. Initially, the *"main audience were industry and employers, combined with friends and family",* though the institution also tried to get children excited about the exhibition *"there were posters done for schools in previous years."* After the first year, the theme changed to a celebration of the students of the institution and not a lot more research has been done since that time.

Indeed, according to EC1, most of the research for this event had been done before the first of its annual presentations, and since then it appears to have evolved rather than having been deliberately planned - *"the institution was looking to get more brand exposure in the market in the first place. There was an existing event within one of the departments and the people responsible thought about creating a bigger event around it including more departments."* Now in its 5th year, the event is still seen as *"a platform to show the quality of work, to support our students",* and to get more exposure in the marketplace while trying to *"piggyback on their [the students'] success as a product the institution is offering."* EC2 noted that the ability to bring in people to experience the quality of work produced by the students is also potentially useful as a means to *"get industries to come along and to promote"* the institution, and to therefore raise brand exposure.

Yet, though there has been some research within the institution, and all members seem to have a clear idea about the purpose of the event, little research appears to have been done outside of the institution. Indeed, EC1 admitted that *"we haven't really talked to the industry on what they want to get out of it. The first two years we tried to include industry and we hired someone to create a big industry database, including all industry people who had some connection with the institution. We tried various ways to attract them but they seem to like to come incognito, to fit in with the rest. A lot of the industry members are former members of our institute."*

4.1.2 The design stage

EP clearly believes that innovative and creative design is a key to a successful event, for his company has only a small number of clients who *"want the same event over and over again."* Most other clients require a different event with the same outcome, and EP argues that events must necessarily be 'different' in order to keep the people excited. However, when a few years ago this might be merely a matter of *"different location or different speakers"*, his contemporary clients are far more budget conscious and insistent on a better outcome. *"In the past, they had a party because they wanted a party. Today people want real outcomes."*

For EC1, the design stage is best seen as the creative process of getting the big picture of an event together, while the approach used towards the design of the event *"depends on who is leading the design side of it. They come up with a few proposed directions and give it to the committee and they agree or disagree on the topic and it processes from there on"*. Believing that it is important to keep the 'why' of an event in mind at the design stage, the event co-ordinator creates *"a brief which really just covers the audience we are aiming for, the core info we want to convey and I guess we revisit the idea of celebrating the success of our students, with an underlying thing we want to convey... we bring it to the first meeting to check if we are on the same page."*

However, this can on occasion become complicated by the influence of the students, for the event co-ordinator needs to work closely with the design studio to ensure that the eventual design is such that all the *"information then comes back together to the committee and decisions are made within that committee, it's really a group decision."* However, *"the design studio usually does its own brainstorming to come up with some possible directions on how to implement the success of the students at the school of design. Sometimes it took quite a long time... a couple of years ago they came up with 10 ideas before we agreed on a theme – so it was quite a long process. Last year we used some of these ideas and threw a couple of other ideas in and we presented 3 themes to the committee and they agreed on one"*.

The design process this year *"started quite visually and we layered the theme on top of that"*, and this is a process that seems to have worked well. EC2 commented *"I haven't really noticed any major challenges which I thought there might be in terms of design, because of the designers in the group, but they have been quite easy to get on with. Challenges would have been mainly the budget and some density of work and how to look at different ways of promotion or trying to get money to do certain things because you have the production rushed."* Indeed, especially in the design and planning stages of the event, the budget was not surprisingly a major concern that was resolved in a circumstance where the event co-ordinator *"found some money from other areas which hasn't been used by other activities and …. some extra from the main marketing budget. But that's probably the struggle really in terms of challenges."*

4.1.3 The planning stage

According to EP, the planning stage is the one at which objectives are translated into operational guidelines, and he notes that the key to a successful event is quite simply *"planning, planning, planning and planning"*. Given that this event is well established in the institution's annual calendar, the basis for specific event planning in this instance lay with the experiences of past years. In this respect EC1 noted that a clear pattern was evident, following on from its original introduction to celebrate the success of the students and to showcase their work to a broad audience. *"In the first two years we had a reasonably good budget that helped to get the wider exposure, in the last two years the budget was reduced quite significantly. We definitely do not get the same cut through but we seem to attract nearly the same numbers."*

EM commented that the design stage of the process usually concentrates on how to transfer the celebration theme to the potential audience, and that it therefore functions as a basic foundation for a planning stage in which this theoretical design is translated into a practical project plan. So is there any form of formally defined framework to guide event planning? According to EP, such an idea is an impossible dream, for *"most events are very different …. what we tend to find is that for individual clients they tend to work with internal frameworks and follow them. For big conferences, the milestones are set by the components – closing of early registration, registration, sponsorship"*. Thus, EP believes that a common operating model for all events will be difficult to establish, but he did acknowledge that a framework of best practice, adjusted to the individual client's wants and needs, might be a possibility.

Indeed, in the current case, there was little or no sign of a formal guiding framework, though EM claimed to be working within a loose framework for the planning of the opening night - *"I am quite logical and I take a simplistic approach to it. I mean it's just a who, what, where, when and how..."* – while acknowledging that *"sometimes that can seem quite vague in one sense."* This is a position that EC1 readily agreed with, suggesting that *"the event manager has a framework for the planning of the night, but not for the event itself."* In addition, EC1 noted that her own planning responsibilities included *"the studio and the graphic side of things, and then I have the committee (the head of department from each of those disciplines). They look after their own work for their group and produce or assimilate that information down .... whereas I am more of the coordinator of the promotion around the event and getting that happening."* Thus, though there is no over-riding framework for the planning of the event, the committee leaders are in charge of the various departments and they are *"working out the themes that were relevant to those areas. This year for example they were talking about releasing the creativity which is the theme for this year."*

Similarly, in a parallel project the event manager was planning at that time, it appeared as if this absence of framework was potentially quite damaging; *"I'm not sure what it is, I'm not sure how much money we've got, I'm not sure how many people we can have involved. You know, lots of stuff ups and maybes. That always seems a bit harder and takes a bit more time... seems a bit more intangible."* In this other event, for example, there is a challenge in getting to the audience they are attempting to reach, because many of the students are on holidays during the proposed time of the event. As such, there is an issue with the exhibition in terms of getting the necessary information to all the students of the departments – one department in particular that has lost a staff member with considerable past experience of managing information flow during the planning stages of the event.

Most other topics that come up during the planning stage are based on past years' experience, for example security. *"We had a lot more security last year. I think it was better and they did a fabulous job with the crowd management plan. So we are sticking with that same security plan this year. The difficulty is the building that we hold it in; there are so many nooks and crannies and ways to get in that building. Unless we have security guards in every single room 24/7 we are never going to solve that problem."* One thief went as far as to *"switch the fire alarms on so the building was evacuated to steal work."*

4.1.4 The co-ordination stage

The approach of the event manager towards events is setting milestones and deadlines for them, and then working through each of these milestones and deadlines as they occur. For EC1, this is a relatively ad hoc process: *"A lot of it would be in my head. The committee would probably be my checkpoint. At each meeting we would have an agenda of things we would have to discuss and following the meeting I send out the actions that have to be done and then we follow up on the things at the next meeting."* While the event co-ordinator is responsible for the overall event, every department would have their own deadlines to ensure that the students are on track. But unless *"it has an impact on the entire event the department will have to deal with it by themselves."*

At this stage in the interviews, respondents then discussed the range of skills and abilities that would turn out to be useful during the management process, with EM being quite clear that these revolved around the maintenance of logic, discipline and pragmatism. EM had significant previous experience in the travel industry, where there is a similar mind set of *"it's what happens next, what happens next..."* Thus, EM's advice is to stay calm during an event, because *"things happen, but who else noticed, who else knows? Just keep that in mind."* On a good day, EM is seeking new ideas by talking to people, thinking outside of the square to come up with new ways of doing things: *"That might be a kind of quirky way that we can promote it or something that we can do for our audience. Because events are usually getting boring after a while."*

For EC1, no formal training has been provided for her role as the key decision maker in overseeing the operation of the event - *"the project came to me as part of my role as marketing account manager."* However, the marketing account manager role did prove useful in terms of more effective planning and decision making. *"I am always involved in some kind of planning, discussing, coordinating for events included in my role. It will involve liaising with departments, and externally, depending on goals."* On a good day, EC1 would plan and progress an idea or plan, and achieve success in getting the people from different departments excited about these. A bad day would be when *"I have to tell someone a bad message",* conveying a message people do not want to hear, or that someone's new idea does not fit into the institutional brand profile. EC1 handles this lack of event training by getting advice from various people, and believes it is a good idea to *"use the expertise of people around you"* and to *"make sure you have a good project team."*

Though this was the first time that EC2 had been associated with this particular event, she had initially studied Marketing and Management, and become involved with the planning of an event that way. *"I found this nicer job 2 years later, and was obviously quite happy to get into the event field. All marketing roles have always been quite forward, which always ties into an event of some description, so I was always organising – whether it was a quiet function or a board room lunch or a seminar on something."* Thus, she has been *"doing events probably for the last 8 years, mostly London and Melbourne. Most of them have been in the corporate sector, so very high end clients. They have been run really well, but always obviously they come into some sort of problems."* For EC2, the lessons from those events are manifold, but the main one is *"to listen to your own advice"* as sometimes you find yourself working with clients who have no event experience – as such, they might have an idea that is not going to work out, but they still push it forward.

Another issue for EC2 is the problem of doing the same event over and over again, and eventually losing the interest of the public. Just because people think that something went well in the past does not mean that we have to stick with it. EC2 believes that this could be avoided by coming up *"with new ideas of how to run the event"* which is what she wants to do with this exhibition. *"I wanted to try something different with the food and as we said before with signage and inside we could do something new."* But we have to get consent within the committee first! As such, her final piece of advice was to *"get an understanding of the different parts of the industry that you're in, know who are involved with it and know what we can bring to the event …. creating stronger relationships with the different people involved so it will all work out and you can go back to them."*

4.1.5 The evaluation stage

As was the case with EM, EP has a significant past experience in the tourism and travel industry. For him, five years into a new job is still very exciting and *"there haven't been two days the same."* However, his post-event evaluations always start with the question of whether the client's goals have been met. *"Is the client happy and did we achieve what the client wanted to achieve."* But even here, there is no standardised framework to evaluate events. For associations and other non-profits, there is always a possibility to *"send out evaluation forms to all attendees",* but corporate event evaluations have to principally rely on the client's feedback to the event manager.

In the case study event however, the desired outcome was actually difficult to summarise, and its level of success therefore difficult to measure. EC1 noted that evaluation of the first event was very intense, as one department had an existing event they were *"passionate about and they took a lot of ownership",* while other departments had never done an event before. EM agreed, saying that *"in the first year that we were involved, we did a big viral campaign, you know… people could vote whether [our students] were hot or not… so that was very tangible because we could see how many people were voting".* However, this evaluation showed that not a lot of people came to the event, and the usefulness of the event was therefore questioned – however, heads of department decided that *"there was value in the event and they were keen to address the issues and to look at ways to do it better the next year."*

In one of the next years, the institution targeted specific audiences by catering for them at mini events. There was a media lunch and an early opening for the industry. But, as EC1 observed, *"it did not really work."* Then *"last year we had an external PR company coming on board and they were very hot on a hosting for the media again. They said let's not host it on a different time but let's build it in the opening but at a separate location."* Again, they failed to attract enough people to make it worthwhile.

In recent years, the primary approach to evaluation has been based on a formal debrief session, and EC1 noted that this was *"broken down with different headings for different components of the event. I put in comments I get from people about the different areas and we look back at them at the beginning of the next event."* At the same time, no real advances have been made in terms of measuring success during the event itself. EM noted that the practice this year had been to *"just rely on numbers coming through the doors which is a guessing game really. We can see the people on the opening night and then we've had other staff members go to the show on a Saturday and say "oh my God the car park was full; there were all of these people there on a Saturday" but you know we don't have someone going and counting all the people coming through the doors. But, at the debrief, the questions I usually ask are what went wrong, what didn't work, what could have been."*

For this particular version of the event, EC2 felt that they had *"had a great response, good feedback about the coordination, the look and feel of the branding and the quality of work."* However, she felt that there were quite a few things that had to change in relation to *"branding, advertisement, billboards – that was a bit of a nightmare",* and this was important as it had caused the event to run over budget. EC2 also believed that better research would have assisted in this respect – given the time over again, *"I would have researched and communicated more with the events team. The catering seemed to be excessive and there are several groups out there who could possibly support us with entertainment."* While EC2 saw potential for improvement in the research, the design part was perceived to be *"quite good. With the budget it was hard to include a lot more."* Overall there could have been more communication and more feedback, and that was singled out for future improvement, but overall the students *"had a great time and enjoyed showing off their work."*

EM summarized the outcome as a *"unique show",* focusing on the great work of the students, though not without issues related to the human element. *"We have humans involved in events and you wouldn't quite know what they're going to do .... we really can only anticipate so much."* On this occasion EM noted that a number of process errors were evident - *"maybe we went too far trying to focus on sustainability and not handing out maps to the people. The bar people came from an outside company, they did not know the building too well."* But for EM, the evaluation process was not so much about finding out what went wrong this time, as it is about generating a list of possibilities to improve the process in the future. *"It's just trying to be constructive to make it a better process and a better event at the end of it."*

4.2 Participant observation

Participant observation was the foremost data collection method used during the book field work, in an attempt to gather information about the planning and execution of the event, the processes and relationships involved, and the outcome of the event. As anticipated at the methodology section, participant observation did take a lot of time and researcher involvement, as the researcher was formally included as a member of the planning committee, and additionally met with the event co-ordinator and the event manager on a regular basis. All of those interactions provided considerable information, and deep insights into the planning of the event, though the event co-ordinator had other daily tasks to attend to and some of the planning for the event happened while working on other tasks, e.g. through e-mails, phone calls and while meeting various people on the floor.

This section of the book is restricted to a summary of the researcher's observations during the monthly event management committee meetings, for this is adequate in terms of giving the reader a broad overview of the happenings during the preparations for the event. Specific observations in terms of the proposed best practice framework will be offered in the following discussion section.

Preliminary meeting

The researcher's participation began through a meeting with the institution's marketing manager on the 18th of May. During that meeting, the research project was outlined and the research methods were explained in depth. After written consent was obtained from senior management at the institution, the event co-ordinator and the event manager were briefed on the project and agreed to participate. A formal e-mail was then sent to all prospective committee members, in which they were asked to raise any issues that they might have concerning the research within one week, but no such issues were raised.

Every event the institution is involved with begins with a marketing communication brief that includes the name of the event, the required tasks and resources, a creative brief (including reasons for the event, audience, and goal of the event) and any additional information that might be required or useful. The marketing communication brief is intended to give everyone a broad overview of the event and to create a basic platform of knowledge that can be built upon. As the case study event is an annual event, the marketing communication brief was quite similar to those used in previous years. It stated the name of the event, and identified the different departments who would participate. The goals of the event were specifically to increase brand exposure and brand awareness for the institution, and special features of the event were the involvement of several different departments working together, the celebration of success for students of the institution, and a highlighting of the historic building in which the event was to take place.

Primary target audiences were industry members, employers, professionals and art enthusiasts, and secondary target audiences were families and friends of the exhibiting students. It was intended that visitors to the event would come because of the exhibition itself, because of the cutting edge nature of the designs on show, and because of the opportunity offered to network with others and to celebrate the success of students. To begin to realise the event, the management committee met on a monthly basis, starting with an initial meeting on 15 July.

Committee meeting 1

The first meeting of the event management committee began with a short discussion of the marketing communications brief. Some members of the group were new to the event, and the event co-ordinator read through all of the points of the list to ensure that everyone was fully aware of what was involved. Feedback from last year's exhibition were discussed, to remind the people of previous key points, and issues such as a shortage of glasses, the parking plan, the limited signage, a meet and great area in the foyer, and wine top ups on the table were comments that fell within the responsibilities of the event co-ordinator and the event manager. Issues such as ambassadors (persons greeting visitors upon their arrival and giving them directions), clear pricing on artwork for sale, and more signage within the departments were comments that department representatives were responsible for. For the time between each meeting and the organisation of the next, the event co-ordinator was responsible for communication between all committee members and for keeping everyone in the loop.

After the feedback session, the main features of the event were discussed. At this stage, the planning focused on the design for the event and the resources needed. The budget for this year's exhibition was significantly smaller than the budget for earlier years, and this was especially challenging for the event co-ordinator as it was mainly affecting the marketing of the opening function. Therefore ideas for the marketing and promotion campaign were collected from the first meeting onwards. The overall design of the event was the responsibility of the institution's graphic designers, who agreed to present their ideas at every committee meeting, and to integrate relevant feedback in the next meetings' presentation. Thus, at this first meeting, ideas about an appropriate slogan for the event were collected - "breaking boundaries", "expect the unexpected", and "swap the hard work for a celebration" were some of the examples the committee was asked to consider.

Committee meeting 2

The second meeting was held on 27 July, and started with a discussion about possible slogans for the event. Current news topics from all around the world were discussed, including the impact of recession and tough times, the concentration on difference, and the creation of one's own future during those times. The involvement of a new department was discussed, and ideas about their contributions towards the opening function were collected in a collaborative manner, before the design department presented three design ideas which had evolved out of the discussions during the first meeting. Feedback and possible alterations were given by the committee members and then discussed extensively.

The atmosphere was slightly chaotic, as some of the designer participants had limited experience with the management of an event and with working within a committee structure. However, the past experience of the event co-ordinator was able to lead the discussions and was therefore able to direct these people through their new tasks.

Committee meeting 3

The third meeting was held on 24 August, and was the shortest of all. The agenda focused on the design presentation, the pre-arranged room allocations, and several ideas for a marketing and promotion campaign. In summary, the designers presented their alternative concepts and all members of the committee agreed on one of the concepts within a few minutes; the event co-ordinator presented her research about advertisement possibilities, including her requests for information and quotes for newspaper ads, billboards, radio ads, promo teams, posters and flyers; and the room allocations were discussed and most people were happy to keep last year's rooms, though the new department wanted to have a look at the building before they would confirm their selection of rooms.

At the end of the meeting, the event co-ordinator announced her resignation from the committee, and that a new event co-ordinator would take over the role as marketing account manager (and therefore as event co-ordinator) from the next meeting onwards.

Committee meeting 4

The new event co-ordinator received an extensive induction into all aspects of the event, and the requirements of her new role, prior to the fourth meeting on 21 September. The agenda for this meeting included approval of the final design concept, budget/marketing activity, communication, and staffing for the opening night. The designers commenced the meeting by presenting ideas they had around the agreed upon design, and what different variations of the design were possible to support the branding of the exhibition. The timings for the opening function were discussed, with all departments asked to give an estimate of their contributions and the timings involved.

This estimate proved quite difficult for the new department, as they had little prior experience with what works and does not work for exhibitions and shows of this type. In addition, the person who was responsible for exhibition planning within the new department resigned from the committee after this meeting and was replaced prior to the next meeting. This issue raised concerns about the new department's ability to contribute on the opening night, but the actual planning of the event was ultimately not affected.

Various marketing and promotional ideas were presented, which then led into a discussion about the implications of opening night. These promotional plans proved to be a contentious topic for discussion, as the new event co-ordinator was not yet fully up to date with all of the details of progress so far. The event manager was identified as the person responsible to organize the catering for the opening, while the event co-ordinator was responsible for all the promotion, marketing and other queries until then. However, it became apparent that the event co-ordinator had other responsibilities with regards to her role as marketing account manager, and had limited time to explore further promotional ideas – however, the option of bringing in further support from elsewhere in the institution was dismissed by the marketing manager, as she was afraid of an increase in the volume of issues to be faced due to there being more voices on the committee. As a result, some promotional ideas that were linked to the support group had to be dismissed (though some could still be continued).

The fourth meeting felt tough and chaotic to most of the participants, as a new event co-ordinator had to assume and understand the budget responsibilities of the previous co-ordinator, and had to answer questions coming from all committee members without necessarily fully understanding the situation.

Committee meeting 5

The fifth meeting was held on 19 October, about one month before the event was scheduled to start. The agenda for this meeting included room confirmation, industry list update, marketing activity update and other issues. At this meeting, final room allocations were made, invites to industry networks were printed and given to departmental managers to mail to their contacts, and catering arrangements were discussed and catering staff approved – an outside school had been asked to cover this area by inviting some of their hospitality trainees to work the event. Security hire was approved to secure the artwork, as some had been stolen in previous years. Finally, the marketing campaign was launched with a dedicated website and Facebook site going live, and supporting radio ads and billboards being introduced in subsequent days.

Committee meeting 6

The sixth and last meeting before the event was held on 2 November, two weeks before the opening night of the event, to make sure that all departments were on the right track and knew about the timing of the event. All responsible people within all participating departments reported on their progress and the challenges they were facing. Some of these challenges were resolved during the meeting and all departments supported each other with material and ideas.

Final timings were reviewed and verified, and the newly introduced department was evaluated as being well on track. To ensure the prospective audience was well informed, the promotion of the event was reviewed with the only real issue being a relatively minor problem with billboard publicity. All other promotions were well under way, the response rate to publicity was up to expectations. Everyone was excited about the opening function of the event.

Opening night

The opening night for the event was 26 November 2009, with an official start time of 5.30pm, and the staff that were to work on the opening night met at 1.00pm to sort out the catering stations, finalise signage and maps, and set up the attendee survey stations.

EM was in charge of the catering station set up, and it was easy to see that there was previous experience at work in this respect. All of the deliveries came to the main entrance of the venue, and EM then organised the distribution of these deliveries to six separate catering stations located throughout the building. While this was in theory a simple task, it did require a considerable amount of time, as many students still working on their installations resulted in a blocking of several corridors and rooms. At this point, EM became agitated when beverages and food arrived at the same time, and everything began to pile up at the entrance – however, with the help of both staff and students, everything was successfully distributed to each station well before the arrival of hospitality students at around 5.00pm.

It was these students' role to look after each of the six catering stations, and the EM was able to give the students a reminder of event timings, and to explain the detailed requirements of the function before splitting the group into six teams to man the six stations.

At about the same time, the graphic designers from the marketing department pasted up maps around the building to help enhance orientation for the visitors, and the two attendee survey stations were set up. Though this was supposedly an easy task, the location of one station directly next to the main entrance meant that staff had to organise locks and a long cable to connect the computer to the nearest network port.

Visitors began to arrive just after 5.00pm, with a constant flow of people between then and 7.00pm. The event's formal opening ceremony, scheduled for 7.00pm, was located just outside a side entrance to the building, and many visitors seemed to need directions to that area as the signage did not seem to be sufficiently clear – catering staff did have some difficulty in giving directions to people, as they themselves were un familiar with the building. The ceremony itself was well attended, and the location became a little crowded. Most of the departmental presentations were well received, although the new department was perhaps not perceived to have done as well as the more experienced others.

The catering stations closed at 8.30pm, and the visitors gradually drifted away after that time.

4.3 Survey results

The survey part of data collection was designed to gain more knowledge about the opinion of visitors, by collecting opinion from a small sample of attendees as a potential representative of all attendees. Two computers were set up to facilitate a self-complete survey, one at the main entrance and one at a widely used back entrance. These computers were quite clearly visible to the audience, and an opportunity to win a $50 shopping voucher for completing a 10 minute survey was included in an effort to increase responses.

One the opening night of the event, what was thought to be a good location for the survey turned out to be a bad one, as the location was very crowded, and the large number of people limited the visibility of the survey stations. Additionally, people who stood in front of the computer to complete the survey did tend to get pushed away by people entering and leaving the building. For future sessions, an attempt was made to relocate survey-computers, but this was unsuccessful due to the limited length of the cables. As a result, the survey did not achieve the targeted 10% response rate, and in fact just 27 people completed a usable response, which of course does mean that the results cannot in any sense be interpreted as a representation of the entire audience. However, replies to some of the questions show a trend that may prove worthy of further investigation.

The first question asked how respondents had heard about the event, with more than one answer being permitted. 67% of respondents had received a personal invite, and 37% had been told about the event by friends. The event website was used by 20% of the respondents, followed by 18% who were invited via Facebook. The billboard and poster campaigns were mentioned by 8% of all respondents.

The second question focused on the level of satisfaction with different parts of the opening night arrangements. Overall satisfaction with the event rated 4.56 out of possible 5, with the opening ceremony, the performances, the friendliness of staff, and the organization of the event all rating at 4.50. Availability of adequate parking was rated noticeably lower at 3.45.

A third question about possible additions to the facilities offered at the exhibition was answered by 19 people. Better parking, and maps to help find the way to the building, was mentioned by four people, with more maps within the building requested by three people and more space to enjoy the exhibition mentioned by two people. The remaining responses could not identify anything additional that they would require.

5. Discussion

The overall aim of this research was to examine how the performance of small scale local events can be improved by using a framework of best practices of event management. This chapter discusses the findings from the interviews, the participant observation process, and the visitor survey, in an attempt to address the overall research question:

To what extent does a theoretical best practices framework, for the effective management of mega-events, provide optimum guidance for the management of small-scale local events in New Zealand?

As discussed during the earlier literature review, an agreed theoretical framework of best practice for event management does not appear to exist. Thus, in order to fully address the topic as prescribed through the sub-questions identified earlier, it has been necessary to use a provisional framework of four pillars of event management, cross referenced to five stages in the event management process. The results of data collection presented in the previous chapter have been presented in line with the five stages of management; the discussion that follows is therefore presented in the light of the previously identified four pillars – time, finance, technology, and human resources.

5.1 The pillar of time

As identified in the original framework, there are two main considerations with regards to time, namely the value of time and the identification of critical path. The organisation of events is generally very time-consuming, and the inclusion of time assessment as part of overhead costs is an important requirement of recommended best practices. Failure to include this consideration prevents event managers from accurately assessing their time, limits their motivation to reduce time wasting activities, and therefore distorts the evaluation of an event.

The management of small-scale events is often undertaken by employees of the sponsoring organisation, and the **value of time** they spend in working on the event is not always factored into the overall event costs. In the case study situation, the event co-ordinator and the event manager were both employed by the institution and were consequently not required to keep formal track of the time they spent on the exhibition – both of these people had many other duties to attend to during the day, and the event was just one of many projects they were planning and executing during that time. As a result, the organisational skills of both EM and EC were tested daily, and tasks did on occasion get mixed up during the course of a day.

During the preparations for this event, EC was the main contact person and source of information for all stakeholders, and requests for information did come in throughout the workday and interrupted the workflow. Especially at the beginning of the planning process, EC was busy with other duties in her role as marketing account manager, as a result of which her contribution to the first meeting of the committee on 15 July was limited to going through last years' notes and preparing a marketing communication brief which was quite similar to the previous year's one. For subsequent committee meetings, EC did always prepare a written agenda to ensure that main topics were discussed during the meetings, and important issues that arose between meetings were e-mailed to committee members for assistance and feedback.

As the planning process moved into the beginning of November, and the marketing plan was being made ready for launch, the workload for EC was enormous. Around 30 substantial event related e-mails reached the office daily and most of these were important enough to require attention on the day. Throughout this period, EC was working autonomously on the marketing campaign, and had no assistant to entrust with any tasks, other than the ability to seek the opinion of committee members where appropriate. This outcome could arguably have been foreseen with better attention to **critical path**, the event management model that identifies all of the tasks included in an event, shows how these tasks are related, and estimates how long the project will take if all dependent tasks can be undertaken one after another. The critical path diagram depicts the earliest and latest possible starting time for each task with regards to other dependencies, and shows when each task will have to be completed without influencing the overall finish time.

In the case study event, the critical path was set according to two main milestones - launch of the marketing campaign and the opening ceremony for the event – with supporting and dependent tasks needing to be finished before each milestone could be regarded as achieved. While this has been common practice at the institution, EM admitted that were unsatisfied possibilities that could have been tackled by doing more research. One example was the potential to promote the school to potential future students, a process which is thought to be most effective around early September – this opportunity was not taken, because the limited research undertaken for the event did not identify this as a promotional opportunity, and therefore there was no September deadline set for the designers to meet for that purpose.

Critical path analysis is one of the most researched and investigated parts of the major event management process, and it is argued that small-scale local events could benefit from the implementation of a 'light' version of the critical path investigation system. As a component of this process, the introduction of a detailed event time frame is proposed to be potentially beneficial, as the overall effectiveness of time scheduling at small-scale events would be improved by the introduction of specific activity time slots that could have been allocated and measured more easily. In addition, had a greater effort been made to accurately measure the cost to the event of EM and EC time, there may have been a possibility to split responsibilities between different people to allow for a more efficient event planning and resource allocation.

5.2 The pillar of finance

Literature review research into best practice within the pillar of finance revealed the existence of three main topics - the overall costs of conduct, sponsorship, and event marketing and promotion.

The **overall costs of conduct** refer to the costs an event company incurs during the course of managing an event, and includes both the costs that can be directly assigned to the event itself, and a proportion of the general overhead associated with operating the business. While this is an obviously important aspect for an event management company, its applicability tends to be more restricted in cases where the sponsoring organisation manages the event itself. In the case study event, the idea of overall costs of conduct was represented by a discrete event budget that did include direct costs of operation but significantly overlooked the application of any general overhead, and the provision of resources seemed to be based on what was available rather than what was needed.

For example, the provisional framework of best practice event management recommends the introduction of special event software for companies working in the event industry, but the case study event was required to rely on off-the-shelf Microsoft Office due to financial limitations to the introduction of special software. Conversely, the salaries of EM, EC, and other school staff working the event were paid by the institution and were not part of the event budget, and this consideration clearly reduced the costs of conduct by a significant amount. Throughout the event management process, there were additional possibilities to charge other accounts for sub-tasks, e.g. the printing of the posters was charged towards the marketing budget and not to the event budget. While this obviously increases the financial viability of the event, it detracts from any accurate assessment of event cost and complicates EC's ability to accurately plan and cost the event marketing campaign.

More importantly, it becomes very difficult to accurately asses the comparative benefits and costs of the event. From the second year of the event onwards, the institution has had an overall objective to increase brand exposure and brand awareness, though resource budgets have continuously been reduced to the point where they are now at about one quarter of the initial level – at the same time, the original goal to create more brand awareness and exposure has remained the same, though this has not been specified in any greater detail. It is suggested that this would be more effectively managed, and the financial outcomes more easily established, if the overall ambition was quantified by the introduction of supporting SMART goals to enhance the assessment of different marketing and promotional tools with regards to their contribution towards overall objectives.

Sponsorship is accepted as an essential part of all major events around the world, and it is widely recognised that companies support and sponsor an event in exchange for public exposure. While in most cases, particularly in the case of major events, the event could not be realized without a sponsor, the case study institution was able to underwrite all of the costs of conduct as discussed above, and the necessity to secure adequate sponsorship was largely absent. Additionally, the public exposure of sponsor products and services may possibly have detracted from the global goal of maximal brand exposure for the institution during the event. Thus though a carefully selected sponsor could have been used to attract more visitors and complement the institution's brand rather than detract from it, these possibilities were not researched as the exhibition was feasible without a sponsor.

For example, one sponsorship possibility was offered by a particular support group that proposed paying for some of the merchandise in exchange for the exposure of their logo on that merchandise. This proposition was refused by the marketing manager, on the grounds that the overall goal of maximal brand exposure could have been compromised, and this may in fact have been a sound decision as that support group were still willing to organize an outside BBQ area and a major energy drink company to sponsor drinks and music in front of the building. The public exposure for this support group was immense, due to a well-chosen location, for most of the approximately 3000 visitors had to walk past the BBQ and entertainment area to enter the exhibition building.

Marketing and promotion are increasingly challenging tasks for events all around the world, and marketers are fighting for attention amongst a steady increase of products and events by using an ever wider mix of communication channels. In this regard though, Gitelson & Kerstetter (2000 in Smith, 2008) have researched the typical information flow found in many events, and concluded that people still use previous experience as the main source of information - if they have no experience they ask friends and family for advice. As a result, Smith (2008) concluded that, for most promotions, past experience was more important than channel effectiveness.

The main advantage held by the case study event is the fact that it has been around for several years, and each year the students invite their families and friends to come along and celebrate with them. Therefore a large group of people with former experience exists, though the institution has retained relatively little information about this group and has no contact platform to communicate with these people. Without the advantage of this type of database platform, EC decided to work with a specialized media company to implement a media marketing campaign, and that company recommended announcements over local radio, print advertisements in various newspapers and magazines, cinema screen ads, bus backs and outdoor advertisements such as billboards.

While a broad range of possibilities was introduced, the relevance for the target audience was not always obvious to the researcher, and it seems reasonable to suggest that the media company could have offered more of their experience to implement a strategic marketing plan that sought out specific target market segments and identified the best ways to reach them. In the end, the sum cost of the recommended marketing activities was approximately three times the available budget, and the suggested options pared right back to two radio announcements, one newspaper and one special magazine ad, and three billboards around the city. All of this was scheduled to launch the marketing campaign on 1 November.

The finally agreed media campaign was supported by various promotions designed to increase the awareness of the event. Promotions included front page event publicity on the institutional website, and a supporting notice on an associated institution's website; creation of a dedicated and event specific website and Facebook group; posters displayed within and around the institution, direct mail invites to key industry contacts, and event-branded t-shirts for staff.

Announcements on the institution's own website and on a supporter's website did not attract a lot of attention, though the event website (designed and built by the institution's IT department) was more successful. Traffic flow monitoring by Google Analytics showed that 527 different people had generated 659 page visits, with 99 different origin sources used to get to the page. The most commonly used were Google searching used by 290 visitors, direct access used by 142 visitors, 87 accesses via Facebook clicks, and 32 visitors referred by nzila.co.nz. Notably though, the Facebook group contained all necessary information about the event and was very popular in the days immediately prior to the opening. Members of this group were encouraged to invite friends to join, and in the end nearly 2000 people had been invited to join the group and come to the exhibition. For a free marketing tool, this was an outstanding success.

The same could not be said for billboard advertising which turned out to be extremely problematic and a time-consuming task for EC. After the initial selection of three suitable sites, the billboard company realized that they already booked one of the sites to another advertiser, with a second pre-booked site given to another advertiser with a higher bid price just before the skins were scheduled to be installed. The media company who were advising EC did not always search for better options for the institution and in one instance EC had called the billboard company and got a better deal than the media company had been able to arrange for the institution. This led to a level of mistrust and frustration between the event co-ordinator and the media company, and an eventually unsatisfactory relationship.

During the installation of the billboards several mistakes were made, and only one billboard was placed in the correct location at the agreed time, while another was place in the wrong location and a third made available two days later than arranged and one billboard was put up on the wrong location. All bill boards were eventually in place as intended four days later than the original schedule. Furthermore, operational problems were experienced with one of the billboards half way through the media campaign, and the overall experience was profoundly unsatisfactory – this may have been a possible reason why the reach of this media was also ineffectual.

In this respect, the researcher's small attendee survey revealed that, while 67% of respondents had been invited to the event, 37% had been informed by friends, 22% used web sources, and 18% used Facebook, just 8% had seen billboards and/or posters. This clearly suggests that, as the literature predicted, the cheaper direct promotion campaign was far more effective than the higher priced media campaign. It may therefore be a good idea for event managers to divert more resources into a boost for the promotional campaign for next year's event, and the use of student expertise and involvement could conceivably generate even more students to boost the promotional campaign next year this campaign has even more potential. These suggestions do need further research, but they do offer some alternative thinking on ways to handle the marketing challenges for small-scale events.

In summary, the establishment of better systems to record contact details and participant feedback, combined with the introduction of a professional lead management system, could allow the institution to greatly enhance communication with former visitors, and to use them as a local information source for people who want to talk with someone who has previously attended the exhibition. Furthermore, it is suggested that the implementation of, and concentration on, SMART marketing and media goals would improve outcomes for the institution. *"Promotional channels such as radio, television, newspapers, magazines, posters and banners, were all significant in raising awareness of the event, but not highly rated as the most important source of information... Media sources tended to be supplementary information sources"* (Smith, 2008, p. 30).

5.3 The pillar of technology

The provisional framework of best practices splits technology into the five categories of code of conduct, location, communication, entertainment, and benchmarking.

Technology is the most time saving tool people have at their disposal, and it is a tool that can be applied to many specific areas of event management. That being the case, theory suggests that an established **code of conduct** can be used within an event company to keep technology up to date and to minimise the workload of event staff. Used appropriately, technology can significantly accelerate processes and store large amounts of data, thus greatly simplifying the work of the event manager. In this respect, Goldblatt (1997) has identified several best practices for event management technology, suggesting that the primary benefits of a code of conduct are realised when acquiring appropriate technology, establishing the technology in collaboration with staff, and reassessing technologies preparatory to scheduled update.

While those best practices may well be relevant for a larger event management company, the issues associated with resource demand and performance complexity pose significant challenges for small-scale events. The level of return on investment needed to justify the high initial investment is difficult to obtain for small-scale events companies, and this is an even greater difficulty for those companies and institutions that are required to plan and implement several small-scale events in house.

As recognized in the best practices framework, the question of **location** is the single most important aspect of every event, and this principle was amply demonstrated during the case study event. Here, though Goldblatt (1997) recommends the implementation of a focus group to evaluate the location from a patrons' perspective, this was deemed impracticable because of the exhibition being spread out throughout the building. This was just one of a range of important and influential features of the location that impacted on the strategies devised:

- Building owned by the institution, so no hire costs
- The year-round home of the design and visual arts staff and students
- A landmark historical building that is well known to industry contacts and the general public
- Inner city location with close public transport
- Ample parking in the institution's own grounds
- Multiple entry and exit ways
- Reasonable disability access (with elevator to upper floor)
- Intricate network of connected small rooms
- Unconstrained overall capacity
- Good toilet facilities
- Three-phase power available
- Previous years equipment available

One quite important drawback of the location is that it does not have a large auditorium, and therefore the opening function was heavily reliant on good weather to the extent that this function could be held outside. Particularly given the vagaries of Auckland, it was surprising to see a total reliance on the advent of good weather, with no apparent contingency plan for use in the case of rain. While the building has no alternative space that could fit the amount of people that came to the opening ceremony, there could (and should) be an alternative plan using several rooms to host the visitors.

With the location comes the issue of parking, with briefing notes from previous years noting that this had been a historical problem. The institution does have enough parking spaces available, but some of the areas are a good walk away, and the roads and pavements are not the best to walk on in exhibition footwear such as high heels. This year, the parking situation was discussed at various meetings and everyone agreed on the provision of more maps and better information services – also discussed were ideas ranging from implementing a parking service to ordering a shuttle bus for at least the opening night. However, as the parking issue was part of EM's responsibility, EC did not proceed on any of the suggested improvements, and EM eventually adopted the same parking plan as had been used in the previous year.

While theoretical best practices ask for the design of good and highly visible parking plans, with VIP parking areas that can be given to important industry contacts, this has not yet been fully absorbed for the case study event. Though the implementation of a formal parking plan in previous years did improve the parking situation significantly, comments from both this and previous years indicate that this is still an issue. While the situation today appears to be a lot better than it was during the first years of the exhibition, there are still more lessons that can be learnt from the framework in this respect.

Inside the building, each department was allocated its own section of rooms, where they could set up for the artworks and temporarily modify the rooms to suit – the rooms had to be re-set to their original layout after the exhibition had concluded – and a branding strategy for the building was organised by the graphic designers who ordered banners, posters, food stickers and floor plans. While the floor plans were good at the beginning of the event, they became less effective as more people arrived and the location became crowded, and a more effective array of floor plans would have enhanced the orientation of visitors and led to a clearer communication of the point of the exhibition.

Even though **communication** is conventionally regarded as a sub-field of the social sciences, many people hold the opinion that communication is better seen as a science in itself. Wars have been fought, marriages have been ended, employees have left, and customers have been lost due to poor communication, and an effective communication strategy is widely regarded as essential for the success of every event. Here, even minor misunderstandings can have a major impact on the outcomes and perceptions of an event, and many of these misunderstandings can be traced back to a breakdown in internal communications, that is in the systems and processes used by event management staff to relate to each other and to other relevant entities within the organisation.

Communication and coordination within and between individual departments was assigned to a single responsible person in each department and, before the first meeting of the committee, the representative of each department had to be identified. This was an informal process, as EC had been working with the departments on a daily basis in her role as marketing account manager. Two of the departments had the same representatives as last year, another department was able to easily identify the appropriate person, and just one department was represented by the head of the department - supposedly until an appropriate representative was found. This did not happen, and the head of department eventually attended all of the committee meetings up until the event itself.

Before each committee meeting, EC sent out e-mails with the agenda for members to prepare for, and the initial marketing communication brief was attached to the first invitation to the 15 July meeting. In addition, irregular meetings were held with the graphic designers to discuss the progress of their work and the next steps to be taken – during these meetings, presentations for the next committee meetings were informally considered and prepared and, especially at the design stage, other issues such as floor plans, posters, billboards and banners also required attention. In each of these meetings, communication was evenly split between the stakeholders of the topics discussed, and discussion proceeded in what seemed to be a fair and reasonable manner.   Main communication channels used between the meetings were e-mails, phone calls, and informal discussions during other unrelated meetings.

EC1 did send out follow-up action plans after the meetings to let everyone know what their tasks were, but EC2 chose to trust the discussions during the meetings to be sufficient to fulfil this task. On one occasion this evaluation proved to be wrong, as one department did not send out invitations to their industry contacts within the discussed timeframe.

In terms of external communication, theory suggests that it is vital to assess and qualify the target audience at the outset of the process, for this is what will determine the communication channels that are appropriate to use to reach out to that audience. In this regard, the three target audiences that had initially been identified in the marketing communication brief were:

- Group 1:   Industry / Employers / Media / Professionals
- Group 2:   Family and friends of the students
- Group 3:   Prospective students

EC handled all of the communication that was involved with the marketing campaign, such as dealing with the media company, requesting all relevant quotes, and organising the information necessary to support the campaign. However, promotional activities were performed by various people – the departments were asked to put together PR articles, the IT manager created the website, and the researcher handled the social media activities. While other people performed these tasks, EC was the main contact person who kept track of progress.

Tasks related to the actual event were dealt with by EM. Her job included organisation of the catering stations and hiring of the band for the entrance area. Though apparently simple, a review of the tasks involved in "organisation of the catering stations" is instructive as an example of the complexity involved:

- Mark the catering station locations on floor plans

- Plan the equipment needed for each catering station

- Plan the refreshments needed

- Get quotes for food and beverages

- Organise staff to man the catering stations

- Hire security to protect the artwork and to implement a traffic plan

- Order the equipment

- Order the food and beverages

- Set up the catering stations on the day of the event

- Induct the catering staff on the day of the event

- Distribute refreshments to the various catering stations throughout the building

- Look after the catering stations during the event

- Break down the catering stations after the event

All the communication that was involved with regard to the tasks above was handled by EM, while most other responsibilities were assigned to EC - including, as has been previously mentioned, the main issues involved in external communication.

One major investment that can easily be justified for events of this nature is the investment in a programme of **entertainment**. Entertainment is a natural part of every event, and people expect to be entertained – even at an exhibition, where people primarily come to enjoy the artwork, there is some expectation of suitable entertainment to enrich the experience and to stimulate all the senses. As such, the provisional best practices framework splits the design of the entertainment element into three parts – analysis of audience to ascertain their tastes, inspection of the location to determine possibilities, and imagination of the entertainment from the guests' perspective.

In the case study event, EC1 had a broad knowledge base about the event based on past experience, and knew that music is the least the audience would expect during the event. Thus, while the artwork was clearly the main attraction for the event, each department had music installed at various sections of the exhibition, thus providing a range of different entertainment options. Some areas had background music playing, while others had a DJ taking care of the music, and EM had hired a band to play at the main entrance area. On the first day of the event, the opening ceremony was followed by the band playing in the main entrance hall. Throughout that time, the six catering stations within the building were opened to offer the guests refreshments, and this was well patronised and appreciated. Though catering staff had maps of the building to help people with their orientation, it might have been beneficial to involve catering staff earlier in the process, and walk them through the entire building to increase their orientation and knowledge of the building. Signs to direct people to the opening function could have been a useful additional service as well.

While music has been a feature of the event since the first year of the exhibition, it has remained largely similar for the years afterwards. While this is mostly due to space characteristics of the location, some future enhancements might nevertheless be possible. For example, people who had just entered the exhibition, and were looking for orientation, were distracted from listening to the band, and in total its efforts were not as much appreciated as they might have been. There may be some potential in using the foyer space as a welcome and orientation area to help guests with the orientation, while the band is playing outside to attract more people from the vicinity. The model could be the airport at Rarotonga, where a local band is playing to welcome international guests onto the island, thus creating a warm atmosphere which gives a positive first impression of local culture before entering the airport building.

Finally, it is important under this pillar to note that the practice of **benchmarking** is still very much in the developing stage within the event industry. Though an important aspect of business management practice worldwide, requiring companies to compare processes, practices, procedures and performances to enhance their performance, it is difficult to compare events with each other because of a clear lack of standardisation. Thus, though comparison with previous years' events gives some indication of the success of the event, this can only ever be an indication, as the both the settings for and the funding of the exhibition have changed significantly. Future investigation of EventsCrop as a potentially useful tool to objectively and systematically measure the overall impact of events might allow comparisons in the future, but at present there is little opportunity for comparison.

5.4 The pillar of human resources

The last of the four pillars of best practices identified in the provisional framework is that of human resources, with the sub-categories of event management, staff, volunteers, and customer relationship management (CRM).

In the case study event, the **management** of the exhibition was predetermined by the positions the people held at the institution. The representatives of the departments, the event manager and the marketing account managers were automatically part of the planning, organizing, leading and controlling team for the event, and it was the role of this management team to set the foundation of the work and to guide the remainder of the event team throughout the process. The quality of their management would obviously establish the foundations for the display of student work, and the better the preparations made, the better subsequent activities could be undertaken by other people arranging their part of the exhibition.

The management of the exhibition was not constant throughout, for EC1 resigned from the organisation in September and was replaced be another person with a different approach to the event. Similarly, the person who was representing the new department taking part in the exhibition for the first time left the institution half way through the planning process, and was replaced by another person. Aside from these disrupts to continuity, it should be remembered that the event management team was challenged by the responsibilities of their substantive positions in the school and, for example, EM was often busy with other tasks and could not always attend meetings. It is in the researcher's view likely that a numerically smaller team with fewer additional responsibilities might have been more effective in researching the overall objective of the event and improving the strategic marketing communication plan.

Staffing is a major issue for an event management team, as it is vitally important to get the right mix of people together to realise events. At small-scale local events, a small team often improves the team spirit, but has to contend with a limited knowledge base from which to retrieve information and source advice. Throughout the event management process, different tasks and new challenges arise daily, and whatever these tasks and challenges may be, the event staff will be required to respond. In this instance, while the event management committee can be seen as 'management' for the purposes of this discussion, the graphic designers, IT manager, merchandise manager, and the researcher can be best seen as 'staff' of the event.

With regards to best practices identified earlier, conscious efforts were made to involve staff in all decisions of the committee, and one major task for EC was consistently keeping in touch with all staff to discuss directional changes agreed to at committee meetings. However, as is common with smaller events where technical expertise is lacking, it was necessary to use externally outsourced staff for two main aspects of the event – catering sourced from a collegial catering school, and security sourced from an external security firm – and this of course added an additional complication to the overall success of the event. While established and reputable suppliers were chosen, the risk here is that, due to time constraints, not enough research into alternative options is conducted – the bets practices recommendation here is that a specific and regular time slot is set aside to ensure that continuous research is conducted and alternatives considered.

For both the catering and security elements of external staffing, EM inducted all personnel and explained their task during a briefing session before the event. While the catering staff was only present on the opening night, getting this aspect of the event right is always a critical issue. For this event, food selection was arranged by a local catering company who were happy to incorporate specially designed labelling on their food products, and the quality of food was excellent though the costs of catering was less well received by the management committee. The school works with this catering company on a regular basis, but several members of the committee would have preferred to get more quotes and arrange for less expensive catering options.

Security was hired to be present throughout the event to ensure that the artwork was safe. This was done in response to a previous instance where the fire alarm was deliberately activated to get the building evacuated to make possible the theft of artwork, and EM worked closely with the security firm to develop several contingency plans that could be implemented in a range of extreme situations. Luckily none of those situations happened during the event. Other vendors included the printing shops that made the banners, posters and floor plans where, after the final design had been approved by the committee, terms of trade were researched in order to get branding material done in a good quality for a good price.

With regards to **volunteer** staff, who are often the very public face of an event in the eyes of attendees, there is little to say as this event was not big enough to actually require the recruitment of volunteers to look after guests. Still, various students volunteered to help set up the different sections of the exhibition, and worked closely with the departments to get their sections ready for the exhibition. This was a great help, not seen by visitors to the function but definitely important, and an investigation into future volunteer opportunities might prove to be worthy of consideration.

The concept of **customer relationship management (CRM)** has to deal with the same issues, though the most important part of the CRM for this event was undertaken in the research stage of the management process, where the target audiences were identified and the marketing activities to target them established. Furthermore, the institution had chosen to manage the exhibition in-house, and therefore EM and both ECs were able to deal with their familiar colleagues. This might prove to be a challenge at other events, as participation in the planning of an event can be seen as an element of job enrichment, and a relevant management issue could arise as a result of new colleagues wishing to become involved with event planning.

Overall, one important aspect of small-scale local event management in New Zealand is that the management and the staff of events usually work closely together, and it is sometimes difficult to distinguish between the two. One reason behind this observation is that New Zealand ranks low in Geert Hofstede's power distance, a consideration that Hofstede introduced during a study on how ethnic culture affects the distribution of values in the workplace. A low power distance reflects a society that emphasizes equality and opportunity for all citizens and has an open communication style, and therefore does not respond well to hierarchies of seniority or the 'power of position.' This was clearly evident in the case study event, and may be an important point of difference if similar studies are carried out in alternative ethnic environments.

5.5 Summary of discussion

The objective of this discussion chapter was to analyse the processes used by the management team throughout this event, with specific regard to the provisional framework of best practices constructed at the conclusion of the literature review – it was necessary to construct this framework to answer the overall research question, because the literature review disclosed that there is no universally agreed framework of best practices in existence. The provisional framework presented suggested best practices in the form of a 5x4 matrix, with the four pillars of time, finance, technology and human resources intersecting with five management processes of research, design, planning, co-ordination and evaluation. This discussion used the four pillars as a structural guideline, and thus discovered some interesting impediments to the increasing success of small-scale events.

One main obstacle towards the implementation and prosecution of any type of management framework is the fact that the institution has no policies in place to guide the extent of preparation required for an event. Any such policy would introduce several processes and guidelines that have to be fulfilled before the next step can be tackled, and these guidelines would be useful in raising awareness and credibility of the event management process.

For example, the main obstruction to the success of the case study event appeared to be the fact that all members of the committee were selected because of their substantive positions within the institution. With the event about half a year away, other daily tasks often seemed more important and always more urgent, and the research stage of the process was ultimately restricted to more or less 'doing what we did last year'. Significant additional research for the event, under various categories as identified in this book, has been identified as an important factor to enhance performance and work more effectively.

The overall strategy for the exhibition was derived from two main objectives, namely an increase in brand exposure and greater brand awareness for the school. In this regard, supporting and complementary SMART goals, supported by the outcome of better research, could have led to more focused actions being undertaken towards achieving these objectives.

Throughout the process of event management, it seemed that preparation for the exhibition was based on a process of dealing with the most obvious next tasks, in a step by step manner and as they became apparent. While dealing with the tasks at hand is always important, the effective management of mega-events requires a structured and well-researched framework that allows evaluation of the importance of each individual task in respect of its contribution to the overall strategy. There appears to be no reason why this model should not directly translate into smaller-scale events.

Turning to the third sub-question of this research, various challenges in small-scale events that are not present in large-scale events have been found. Next to the various other tasks that committee members had to attend to daily, more event software could have made a big difference in the preparations for, and communication of, the event. While mega-events have not only the ability to fall back upon the specialist knowledge that exists within the event team, they can also tap into an extensive network of sponsors and partner firms. Most of these contacts have several years of experience within the event industry, and many contacts outside of the event itself, and it is standard practice for repetitive mega-events to use the experiences of past sponsors and their lead management systems to communicate with possible visitors to events. Additionally, those events are often backed by local government, which can in turn provide more options with regards to the marketing and promotion of events. Greater involvement of the local community that surrounds the case study institution could be a useful first step in this respect.

The fourth sub-question deals with the lessons small-scale event managers can learn from the experience of major events. Several ways of using the lessons from major events, as summarized in the provisional framework of best practices, have been depicted throughout the discussion part. As the following chapter will demonstrate, working towards a strategic orientation within such a framework of best practices is predicted to give the institution a far superior outcome for the resources it needs to invest to make the event a success.

6. Conclusion

The research described in this book has been focused on an evaluation of a potential framework of best practices for the management of small-scale local events, and has attempted to address the overall research question:

To what extent does a theoretical best practices framework, for the effective management of mega-events, provide optimum guidance for the management of small-scale local events in New Zealand?

To answer this research question, four supporting sub-questions were introduced at the beginning of the research process, and were subsequently used as a guideline throughout the book:

- To what extent does an agreed theoretical framework exist to guide the management of large-scale special events?
- To what extent has this framework been tested across a variety of settings?
- What specific challenges are evident in small-scale events that are not present in large-scale events?
- What lessons can managers of small events learn from the experiences of major events?

In terms of sub-questions 1 and 2, the literature review revealed that there does not in fact appear to be any universally agreed theoretical framework to guide the management of large-scale special events, and this negative answer to sub-question 1 did of course mean that sub-question 2 was largely irrelevant. If there is no readily acknowledged framework, no framework exists to be tested.

Therefore, to help answer sub-questions 3 and 4, a provisional framework of best practices was derived from the literature review and depicted as a 5x4 matrix in which the four pillars of time, finance, technology and human resources were cross-referenced to the five management processes of research, design, planning, co-ordination and evaluation. This framework was introduced to allow for a structured discussion of the last two sub-questions, and to subsequently answer the overall research question. The primary conclusions reached as a result of this process are presented in bullet point format below.

- The most important learning that occurred during this event was the importance of having an overall strategy based on extensive research and SMART goals. Especially within the finance and technology pillars, better research would help enhance the performance of the exhibition and would also use the budget more cost-effectively. SMART goals would also give the committee greater guidance, and improve its ability to assess current case by case decisions according to a consistent strategy – only if the case will benefit compliance with the strategy it should be pursued.

- For the effective implementation of strategy, it is necessary that school management puts policies in place to ensure that research is done consistently and that support staff by providing adequate time and sufficient resources to do the research. In both cases, the consistent support and commitment of top management is essential.

- Appropriate recognition of the responsibilities involved in event management should lead to the appointment of a smaller event management team that is better resourced in terms of both time and more tangible resources. While mega events have usually one event manager who makes virtually all of the decisions with regards to event strategy, the exhibition had a relatively large committee to make those decisions. Perhaps as a result of the low power distance referred to by Hofstede, there is a culture of collaboration in New Zealand that can see decision making turn into a long process that involves hearing everyone's opinion before reaching a common agreement. While this ensures the involvement of all stakeholders, it might again be preferable to agree on an overall strategy at the beginning of the process, and then evaluate subsequent personal opinions by their contribution towards the strategy.

- The overall communication strategy needs to improved in order to extract much greater levels of information from currently funded processes. For this exhibition, EC had prepared invitations to be sent out from all departments to their industry contacts but, while more than 3000 invitations were sent out, little is known about the quality of these contacts or the extent of their response. Therefore, the introduction of a professional lead management system would not only be beneficial for the event, but for the wider communication activities of the institution as well.

- Creation of a communication platform through establishment of an online forum for committee members only would give the event co-ordinator the chance to distribute information more quickly and accurately. However, this would require the initiative of committee members in accessing the platform and contributing their ideas – but would remove the need to wait for the next committee meeting and would therefore accelerate the decision-making process.

- An important part of the communication strategy should also be a resolve to work more closely with the surrounding community. This may include places where the local community meets, such as churches, libraries, community centres, etc., and could also include more communication with local businesses, support groups and politicians to gain their support and tap into their network of contacts. The design and visual arts community is another potential driver of greater success for the exhibition, and the marketing campaign could be more effective in enhancing brand exposure to pertinent members of this community by focusing more strongly on their gathering places and areas where they live.

Because no formally defined framework for the effective management of mega-events exists, and because therefore there is little to be learned here for the management of small-scale local events in New Zealand, a provisional framework of best practices was introduced to provide guidance for the planning of such events in New Zealand. The framework proposed here gives the manager of local events the opportunity to learn from the experience of mega-events without making the same mistakes the organisers of mega events have made in the past. As such, it can be seen as a learning tool to increase the performance of local events, and also as an invitation to add personal experiences to the framework to collaboratively enhance its quality and value.

The framework of best practices introduced during this research is a compendium of the literature relating to best practices in various elements of events. It is clearly not yet in a position to provide optimal guidance to event managers, but it is suggested to have potential value in creating an opportunity for small-scale local events in New Zealand to learn from the experiences and mistakes that mega-events have had to experience in the past. Or as Eleanor Roosevelt said: "Learn from the mistakes of others. You can't live long enough to make them all yourself."

7. References

Allen, J., O'Toole, W., Harris, R., & McDonnell, I. (2008). *Festival & Special Event Management* (4 ed.). Milton, Australia: John Wiley & Sons Australia, Ltd.

Arcodia, C., & Barker, T. (2003). *The Employability Prospects of Graduates in Event Management: Using Data from Job Advertisements*. Paper presented at the Riding the Wave of Tourism and Hospitality Research, CAUTHE.

Arcodia, C., & Reid, S. (2002). The Mission of Event Management Associations. In K. Woeber (Ed.), *City Tourism*. Vienna: Springer.

Arcodia, C., & Robb, A. (2000). A Future for Event Management: A Taxonomy of Event Management Terms. In J. Allen, R. Harris, L. K. Jago & A. Veal (Eds.), *Events Beyond 2000: Setting the Agenda* (pp. 154-160). Sydney: Australian Centre for Event Management.

Bamberger, J. (1997). Essence of the Capability Maturity Model. *IEEE Computer, 30*(6), 112-114.

Bartholomew, D. (2002). Event Management : Hype or Hope? *Industry Week/IW, 251*(4), 29.

Baum, T., & Lockstone, L. (2007). Volunteers And Mega Sporting Events: Developing A Research Framework. *International Journal of Event Management Research, 3*(1).

Beaven, Z., & Laws, C. (2008). Never let me down again. In M. Robertson & F. Frew (Eds.), *Events and Festivals*. New York: Routledge.

Bell, C. (1969). A Note on Participant Observation. *Sociology, 3*(3), 417-418.

Bilton, C., & Laery, R. (2002). What can managers do for creativity? Brokering creativity in the creative industries *International Journal of Cultural Policy 8*(1), 49-64.

Borrego, M., Douglas, E. P., & Amelink, C. T. (2009). Quantitative, Qualitative, and Mixed Research Methods in Engineering Education. *Journal of Engineering Education, 98*(1), 53-66.

Carr, L. T. (1994). The strengths and weaknesses of quantitative and qualitative research: what method for nursing? *Journal of Advanced Nursing, 20*(4), 716-721.

Cassell, C., Bishop, V., Symon, G., Johnson, P., & Buehring, A. (2009). Learning to be a Qualitative Management Researcher. *Management Learning, 40*(5), 513-533.

Catherwood, D. W., & Van Kirk, R. L. (1992). *Special Event Management*. New York: John Wiley & Sons, Inc.

Cheney, G., Christensen, L., Zorn, T., & Ganesh, S. (2004). *Organizational Communication in an Age of Globalisation*. Prospect Heights, IS: Weveland Press.

Clarke, A. (2004). *Evaluating mega-Events : A critical review*. Paper presented at the 3rd DeHaan Tourism Management Conference "The Impact and Management of Tourism-Related Events". University of Nottingham, UK.

Clifton, J. (2009). The Next Generation of Leadership. *Journal*. Retrieved from http://gmj.gallup.com/content/124079/Next-Generation-Leadership.aspx#2

Collis, J., & Hussey, R. (2003). *Business research: A practical guide for postgraduate and undergraduate students*. New York: Palgrave Macmillan.

Cormack, D. (1991). *The Research Process in Nursing* (Vol. 2). Oxford: Blackwekk Scientific.

Darling, R. B. (1998). The Value of a Pre-Internship Observation Experience. *Teaching Sociology, 26*(4), 341-346.

Davies, J., & Brown, L. (2000). Tourism: Food, Wine and Festivals - a delectable mix. In R. Harris, J. Allen, L. K. Jago & A. Veal (Eds.), *Events Beyond 2000: Setting the Agenda* (pp. 161-170). Sydney: Australian Centre for Event Management.

DeMunck, V. C., & Sobo, E. J. (1998). *Using methods in the field: a practical introduction and casebook*. Walnut Creek, CA: AltaMira Press.

DeWalt, B. R., & DeWalt, K. M. (2002). *Participant observation: a guide for fieldworkers*. Walnut Creek, CA: Alta Mira Press.

Duffy, M. E. (1987). Methodological triangulation a vehicle for merging quantitative and qualitative methods. *Image, 19*(3), 130-133.

Erber, S. (2002). *Eventmarketing: Erlebnisstrategien für Marken; Innovative Konzepte, zahlreiche Fallbeispiele, viele Tipps zur Umsetzung in der Praxis* (Vol. 3). Munich: Redline Wirtschaft bei Verlag Moderne Industrie.

Event. (2009). Event. 2009. In myethomology online dictionary. Retrieved from www.myethomology.com.

Fabling, R. B., & Grimes, A. (2007). Practice Makes Profit: Business Practices and Firm Success. *Small Business Economics, 29*(4), 383-399.

Getz, D. (1998). Information Sharing Among Festival Managers. *Festival Management & Event Tourism, 5*(1), 33-50.

Getz, D. (2000a). Defining the Field of Event Management. *Event Management, 6*(1), 1-4.

Getz, D. (2000b). Developing a Research Agenda for the Event Management Field. In J. Allen, R. Harris, L. K. Jago & A. Veal (Eds.), *Events beyond 2000*. Sydney: Australian Centre for Event Management.

Getz, D. (2007). *Event Studies*. Oxford: Elsevier Ltd.

Getz, D., & Wicks, B. (1994). Professionalism and Certification for Festival and Event Practitioners: Trends and Issues. *Festival Management & Event Tourism, 2*, 103-109.

Gold, R. L. (1958). Roles in sociological field observations. *Social Forces, 36*, 217-223.

Goldblatt, J. (1997). *Special Events - Best Practices in Modern Event Management* (2 ed.). New York: John Wiley & Sons, Inc.

Goldblatt, J. (2000). A Future For Event Management: The Analysis Of Major Trends Impacting The Emerging Profession. In J. Allen, R. Harris, L. K. Jago & A. Veal (Eds.), *Events Beyond 2000: Setting the Agenda*. Sydney: Australian Centre for Event Management.

Goldblatt, J. (2005). *Special Events: event leadership for a new world* (4 ed.). New Jersey: John Wiley and Sons.

Gorgievski, M. J., Bakker, A. B., Schaufeli, W. B., van der Veen, H. B., & Giesen, C. W. M. (2009). Financial problems and psychological distress: Investigating reciprocal effects among Business owners (Publication., from Ingenta: Journal of Occupational and Organizational Psychology:

Hara, K. (1995). Quantitative and qualitative research approaches in education. *Education, 115*(3), 351.

Harris, R., Jago, L., Allen, J., & Huyskens, M. (2000). A Rearview Mirror and a Crystal Ball: Past, Present and Future Perspectives on Event Research in Australia. In J. Allen, R. Harris, L. K. Jago & A. Veal (Eds.), *Events Beyond 2000: Setting the Agenda*. Sydney: Australian Centre for Event Management.

Harris, R., & Jago, L. K. (1999). Event Education and Training in Australia: The Current State of Play. *Australian Journal of Hospitality Management, 6*(1), 45-51.

Haug, C., & Teune, S. (2008). Identifying Deliberation in Social Movement Assemblies: Challenges of Comparative Participant Observation. *Journal of Public Deliberation, 4*(1), 1-37.

Hede, A.-M., Jago, L. K., & Deery, M. (2002). *Special event research 1990-2001 : Key trends and issues. In Australian Centre for Event Management (Ed.).* Paper presented at the Events & Place Making: Event Research Conference. University of Technology Sydney.

Hiller, H. (1995). Conventions as mega-events. A new model for convention-host city relationship. *Tourism Management, 16*(5), 375-379.

Hiller, H., & DiLuzio, L. (2004). The Interviewee and the Research Interview: Analysing a Neglected Dimension in Research. *Canadian Review of Sociology & Anthropology, 41*(1), 1-26.

Hinch, T. D., & Higham, J. E. S. (2001). Sport Tourism: a Framework for Research. *International Journal of Tourism Research, 3*(1), 45-58.

Holzbauer, U., Jettinger, E., Knauss, B., Moser, R., & Zeller, M. (2003). *Eventmanagement : Veranstaltungen professionell zum Erfolg führen* (Vol. 2). Berlin: Springer.

Jones, C. (2001). Mega-events and host-region impacts: Determining the true worth of the 1999 Rugby World Cup. *International Journal of Tourism Research, 3*, 241-251.

Kawulich, B. B. (2005). Participant Observation as a Data Collection Method. *Forum: Qualitative Social Research, 6*(2), 1-22.

Kelle, U. (2006). Combining qualitative and quantitative methods in research practice: purposes and advantages. *Qualitative Research in Psychology, 3*(4), 293-311.

Kim, S. S., & Petrick, J. (2005). Residents' perceptions on impacts of the FIFA 2002 World Cup: the case of Seoul as a host city. *Tourism Management, 26*, 25 - 38.

Kolaja, J. (1956). A Contribution to the Theory of Participant Observation. *Social Forces, 35*(2), 159-163.

Lee, C.-K., Lee, Y.-K., & Lee, B. K. (2005). Korea's destination image formed by the 2002 World Cup. *Annals of Tourism Research, 32*, 839-858.

Lindlof, T., & Taylor, B. (2002). *Qualitative communication research methods* (Vol. 2): Thousand Oaks, CA: Sage

Loos, P., Hermes, B., & Thomas, O. (2008). Reference Model-Based Event Management. *International Journal of Event Management Research, 4*(1), 38-57.

Malhotra, D. S. (2002). Successful event management (Book). *Journal of Services Research, 2*(2), 179.

Management. (2009). Management. 2009. In myethomology online dictionary. Retrieved from www.myethomology.com.

Marshall, C., & Rossman, G. (1989). *Designing qualitative research.* Newbury Park, CA: Sage.

Mc Cabe, V. (2001). Career Paths and Labour Mobility in the Conventions and Exhibitions Industry in Eastern Australia: Results from a Preliminary Study. *International Journal of Tourism Research, 3*(6), 493-499.

Mc Donald, I., Allen, J., & O'Toole, W. (1999). *Festival and Special Events Management.* Sydney: Wiley and Sons, Australia.

Merriam, S. B. (1998). *Qualitative research and case study applications in education.* San Francisco: Jossey Bass Publishers.

Meusburger, P., Funke, J., & Wunder, E. (2009). *Milieus of Creativity* (Vol. 2). Netherlands: Springer.

Neale, M. (2000). Time for a new school of thought on degrees. *Marketing Event, 1*(3), 7.

Nelson, K. B. (2004). *Sociological Theories Of Career Choice: A Study Of Workers In The Special Events Industry.* University of Nevada, Las Vegas.

Nichols, D. (2003). Examples of Excellence. *The Meeting Professionals, 23*(10).

O'Toole, W. J. (2000). Towards the Integration of Event Management Best Practices by the Project Management Process. In J. Allen, R. Harris, L. K. Jago & A. Veal (Eds.), *Events Beyond 2000: Setting the Agenda* (pp. 86-92). Sydney: Australian Centre for Event Management.

O'Toole, W. J., & Mikolaitis, P. (2002). *Corporate Event Project Management.* New York: John Wiley & Sons, Inc.

Olum, Y. (2004). *Modern Management Theories and Practices.* Paper presented at the 15th East African Banking Course.

Participant observation in logistics research: Experiences from an RFID implementation study. (2007). *International Journal of Physical Distribution & Logistics Management, 37*(2), 148-163.

Perry, M., Foley, P., & Rumpf, P. (1996). Events Management: An Emerging Challenge in Australian Higher Education. *Festival Management & Event Tourism, 4,* 85-93.

Poggenpoel, M., Myburgh, C. P. H., & Van Der Linde, C. (2001). Qualitative Research Strategies as Prerequisite for Quantitative Strategies. *Education, 122*(2), 408.

Ralston, L. S., Ellis, G. D., Compton, D. M., & Lee, J. (2007). Staging Memorable Events And Festivals: An Integrated Model Of Service and Experience Factors. *International Journal of Event Management Research, 3*(2), 24-38.

Rath, T., & Conchie, B. (2009). Finding Your Leadership Strengths. *Gallup Management Journal, 12-2008,* 73.

Riley, D. M., Newby, C. A., & Leal-Almeraz, T. O. (2006). Incorporating Ethnographic Methods in Multidisciplinary Approaches to Risk Assessment and Communication: Cultural and Religious Uses of Mercury in Latino and Caribbean Communities. *Risk Analysis: An International Journal, 26*(5), 1205 - 1221.

Ross, M. M., Rideout, E. M., & Carson, M. M. (1994). The Use of the Diary as a Data Collection Technique. *Western Journal of Nursing Research, 16*(4), 414-425.

Royal, C. G., & Jago, L. K. (1998). Special Event Accreditation: The Practitioners' Perspective. *Festival Management & Event Tourism, 5,* 221-230.

Schneiderhahn, M. (2002). Some Words to Remember and Live By. *Foundation, 43*(6), 1-3.

Shanka, T., & Taylor, R. (2004). A Correspondence Analysis Of Sources Of Information Used By Festival Visitors *Tourism Analysis, 9,* 55-62.

Silvers, J. R. (2003). Event Management: Profession or Occupation (Publication., from ISES:

Silvers, J. R., Bowdin, G. A. J., O'Toole, W. J., & Nelson, K. B. (2006). Towards an International Event Management Body of Knowledge (EMBOK). *Event Management, 9,* 185-198.

Šindlárová, J. (1999). The research method for contemporary villages: participant observation. *Zemedelská Ekonomika 45*(1), 33-37.

Smith, K. A. (2008). The Information Mix For Evens: A Comparison Of Multiple Channels Used By Event Organisers And Visitors. *International Journal of Event Management Research, 4*(1), 24-37.

Strategic business plan. (1993). Melbourne: Tourism Victoria.

Strategic business plan 1997 - 2001. (1997). Melbourne: Tourism Victoria.

Stylianou, S. (2008). Interview Control Questions. *International Journal of Social Research Methodology, 11*(3), 239-256.

Thompson, K., & Schofield, P. (2002). Towards a Framework for the Study of Overseas Visitors' Travel Behaviour in Cities. In K. Woeber (Ed.), *City Tourism 2002*. Vienna: Springer.

Tools for Creating and Measuring Value. (2007). *Journal of Accountancy, 204*(5), 58-58.

Tope, D., Chamberlain, L. J., Crowley, M., & Hodson, R. (2005). The Benefits of Being There. *Journal of Contemporary Ethnography, 34*(4), 470-493.

Tum, J., Norton, P., & Wright, N. J. (2006). *Management of Event Operations*. Oxford: Elsevier Ltd.

Turner, S. (2009). Participant Observation: A fieldwork technique. *Geography Review, 22*(4), 24-25.

8. Appendices

Appendix 1: A Checklist for Site inspection

Site Inspection Checklist Criteria

Amenities

1. Ability to display banner in prominent location.

2. Limousines for VIPs.

3. Upgrades to suites available.

4. Concierge or VIP floors.

5. Room deliveries for entire group upon request.

6. In-room television service for special announcements.

7. Personal letter from venue manager delivered to room.

8. Complimentary parking for staff or VIPs.

9. Complimentary coffee in lobby.

10. Complimentary office services for staff such as photocopying.

Americans with Disabilities Act

1. Venue has been modified and is in compliance.

2. New venue built in compliance with act.

3. Modifications are publicized and well communicated.

Capacity

1. Fire marshall approved capacity of venue for seating.

2. Capacity of venue for parking.

3. Capacity for exposition booths.

4. Capacity for storage.

5. Capacity for truck and vehicle marshaling.

6. Capacity for pre-event functions such as receptions.

7. Capacity for other functions.

8. Capacity for public areas of venue such as lobbies.

9. Size and number of men's and women's rest rooms.

Catering

1. Full-service, venue-specific catering operation.

2. Twenty-four-hour room service.

3. Variety of food outlets.

4. Concession capability.

5. Creative, tasteful food presentation.

Site Inspection Checklist Criteria *(continued)*

Equipment

1. Amount of rope (running feet) and stanchions available.

2. Height, width, and colors available for inventory of pipe and drape.

3. Height, width, and skirting colors available for platforms for staging.

4. Regulations for use and lift availability for aerial work.

5. Adequate number of tables, chairs, stairs, and other equipment.

Financial

1. Complimentary room ratio.

2. Guarantee policy.

3. Daily review of folio.

4. Complimentary reception or other services to increase value.

5. Function room complimentary rental policy.

Location/Proximity

1. Location of venue from nearest airport.

2. Distance to nearest trauma facility.

3. Distance to nearest fire/rescue facility.

4. Distance to shopping.

5. Distance to recreational activities.

Medical/First Aid

1. Number of staff trained in CPR, Heimlich maneuver, and other first aid.

2. Designated first-aid area.

3. Ambulance service.

Portals

1. Size and number of exterior portals.

2. Size and number of interior portals including elevators.

3. Ingress and egress to portals.

Registration

1. Sufficient well-trained personnel for check in.

2. Ability to provide express check-in for VIPs.

3. Ability to distribute event materials at check in.

4. Ability to display group event name on badges or buttons to promote recognition.

5. Effective directory or other signs for easy recognition.

Site Inspection Checklist Criteria *(continued)*

Registration

1. Sufficient well-trained personnel for check in.

2. Ability to provide express check-in for VIPs.

3. Ability to distribute event materials at check in.

4. Ability to display group event name on badges or buttons to promote recognition.

5. Effective directory or other signs for easy recognition.

Regulations

1. Designation of a civil defense venue to be used in emergencies.

2. Pre-existing prohibitive substance regulations.

3. Other regulations that impede your ability to do business.

4. Fire code requirements with regard to material composition for scenery and other decoration.

5. Local fire officials' requirements for permission to use open flame or pyrotechnic devices.

6. Requirement regarding the use of live gasoline-powered motors.

7. Policy regarding live-trained animals.

Safety and Security

1. Exterior and interior walkways are well lit.

2. Venue has full-time security team.

3. Communications system in elevators is in working order.

4. Venue has positive relationship with law enforcement agencies.

5. Venue has positive relationship with private security agencies.

6. Fire sprinklers controlled per zone or building-wide. Individual zone can be shut off, with a fire marshall in attendance, for a brief effect such as pyrotechnics.

7. Alarm system initially silent or it immediately announces a fire emergency.

8. Condition of all floors (including the dance floors).

Sleeping Rooms

1. Sufficient number of singles, doubles, suites, and other required inventory.

2. Rooms in safe, clean, working order.

3. Amenities such as coffee makers and hair dryers available upon request.

4. Well-publicized fire emergency plan.

5. Balcony or exterior doors properly secured.

Site Inspection Checklist Criteria *(continued)*

Utilities

1. Electrical power capacity.

2. Power distribution.

3. Working on-site reserve generator (and a backup) for use in the event of a power failure.

4. Responsible person for operation of electrical apparatus.

5. Sources for water.

6. Alternative water source in case of disruption of service.

7. Separate billing for electricity or water.

Weight

1. Pounds per square foot for which venue is rated.

2. Elevator weight capacity.

3. Stress weight for items that are suspended such as lighting, scenic, projection, and audio devices.

(Goldblatt, 1997, pp. 50-53)

Appendix 2: Music and Entertainment Terms

Music and Entertainment Terms

Act: A self-contained, rehearsed performance of one or more persons.

Agent: An individual who represents various acts or artists and receives a commission from the buyer for coordinating the booking.

Amateur: A musician or entertainer who does not charge for their services usually due to lack of professional experience.

Arrangements: Musical compositions arranged for musicians.

Band: A group of musicians who perform contemporary music as in rock 'n' roll, jazz, or big band.

Booking: A firm commitment by a buyer of entertainment to hire an act or artist for a specific engagement.

Combo: A musical ensemble featuring combined instruments (usually piano, base, and drums).

Commission: The percentage received by the agent when booking an act or artist.

Conductor: An individual responsible for directing/conducting the rehearsal and performance by musicians.

Contractor: An individual or organization that contracts musicians and other entertainers. This person handles all of the agreements, payroll, taxes, and other employment tasks.

Cover song: A tune popularized by another artist performed by a different artist or group.

Doubler: A musician who plays two or more instruments during a performance.

Downbeat: The cue given by the conductor to the musicians to begin playing.

Drum roll: A rolling percussive sound used for announcements and to create a suspenseful atmosphere.

Drum riser: A small platform used to elevate the drummer above the other musicians.

Duo: An act with two persons. Also known as a double.

Fanfare: A musical interlude used to signal announcements of awards or introductions. Usually includes horns but not always.

Fife and drum corp: A small or larger musical ensemble featuring fifes and drums playing music from the eighteenth century.

Horn section: A group of musicians that specializes in wind instruments and is usually part of a larger ensemble.

Leader: An individual who organizes and conducts a musical or entertainment group.

Manager: An individual who provides management services to an artist, act, or several artists and acts. The manager normally handles all logistics including travel and negotiates on behalf of the artist or act. The manager is paid by the act or artist from fees that are earned through performing.

Marching band: A musical ensemble usually comprised of percussion, horns, woodwinds, and other instruments that play and march simultaneously.

Minimum: The minimum number of hours musicians must be paid.

Octet: A musical ensemble comprised of eight musicians.

Overture: The music performed before the actors or entertainers enter the stage. Also known as pre-show music.

Professional: A musician or entertainer paid for their services.

Quartet: A musical ensemble comprised of four persons.

Quintet: A musical ensemble comprised of five persons.

Road manager: The individual who travels with an act or artist and handles all logistical arrangements.

Sextet: A musical ensemble comprised of six persons.

Sideman/men: Musicians within a musical ensemble who accompany an artist.

Single: An act with one person.

Soloist: A single performer.

Stage manager: An individual who coordinates the technical elements for the act or artist, cues the performer, and provides other services to support the performance.

Stand: The music stand used to hold sheet music.

Top Forty: The top forty musical compositions/recordings selected by *Billboard* magazine. A top forty band is able to perform these selections.

Trio: A musical ensemble comprised of three persons.

Walk-in, walk-out music: Live or recorded music played at the start and end of an event as guests enter or leave the venue.

Walk music: Live or recorded music played as award presenters, speakers, and recipients enter or exit the stage area.

Windjammers: The slang name for circus musicians (mostly horn players).

(Goldblatt, 1997, p. 206)

Appendix 3: Decor Checklist

Decor Checklist

1. What will the venue (site, building) allow in terms of interior/exterior decor?

2. What are the policies regarding installation? What are the policies or laws of the local municipality regarding decorating materials?

3. What is the purpose of the decor?

4. Are you conveying a specific theme?

5. Is there a specific message?

6. What period or style are you attempting to represent?

7. What are the demographics and psychographics of your attendees?

8. Are they spectators or participants?

9. What are the budgetary guidelines for the decor?

10. How long will it be in use?

11. Which existing scenic pieces can be modified to fit your theme or convey your message?

(Goldblatt, 1997, p. 89)

Appendix 4: Logistics

Logistics Laws for Effective Catered Events

1. Determine in advance the goals and objectives of the catered event and match the logistical requirements to these objectives. For example, a brief networking event should use fewer chairs and tables to allow the guests time to mix and mingle with numerous individuals.

2. Determine the ages and types of guests and match the requirements to their needs. For example, if the guests are older more chairs may be needed to provide additional comfort during an extended reception.

3. Identify the food preparation and other staging areas and ensure that there is a clear passageway to the consumption area. Check the floors to make sure they are free of debris and allow the service staff to move quickly.

4. Whenever possible use a double buffet style for this type of service. The double buffet not only serves twice as many guests but also allows the guests to further interact with one another as they receive their food.

5. Do not place food stations in areas that are difficult to replenish. Large crowds of guests may prevent service personnel from efficiently replenishing food stations.

6. When passing food items place a few servers at the entryway in order that guests visibly notice that food is available. It is easy for servers to disappear in a large crowd and this technique ensures that most guests will see and consume at least one of the food items being offered.

7. Use lighting to highlight buffets, carving, and other stations. Soft, well-focused lighting directs the guests' eyes to the food and makes it easier to find as well as more appetizing.

8. Use servers at the entryway to pass drinks rapidly to guests as they enter, or open the bars at the furthest distance from the entrance first. Smaller events with ample time may benefit from passing drinks; however, larger events where the guests must be served quickly may benefit from the bar staging scenario. Once the distant bars begin to experience lines of ten or more persons, open succeeding bars working your way toward the entryway.

9. Instruct the bar captain to close all bars promptly at the appointed time. Use servers to line up at the entryway to assist in directing guests into the main function room.

10. Provide return tables to accept glassware as guests transition into the next event. Carefully staff these areas to avoid too many glasses accumulating.

11. Request that servers distribute any welcome gifts or programs during the set-up period and be staged in each dining station to assist with seating. Servers should be requested to offer chairs to guests without hesitation to expedite seating.

12. Use an invocation, moment of silence, or a simple "bon appetit" to cue guests to begin the meal.

13. The following service times should typically be used for catered events.
    Cocktail reception: Thirty minutes to one hour.
    Seated banquet: One to two hours.
    Preset salad consumption and clearing: fifteen to twenty minutes.
    Entree delivery, consumption, and clearing: twenty to forty minutes.
    Dessert delivery, consumption, and clearing: fifteen to twenty minutes.
    Coffee and tea service: ten to fifteen minutes.

14. Make certain all service personnel have exited the function room prior to speeches or the program. If this is not possible, make certain front tables have been served and that servers only continue service as quietly as possible in back of the function area.

15. Request that servers stand at exit doors and bid guests good-bye and distribute any parting gifts from host/hostess.

(Goldblatt, 1997, p. 160)

Appendix 5: Interview Questions

Pre-interview questions:

The pre-interview questions were split into three main parts: Strategy, lessons learned from last year and skills needed for the event.

Strategy:
- How do you get your clients?
- What are the three main questions you're asking your clients
- Why is the institution organizing the exhibition?
- What is the desired outcome of the exhibition (for the institution, the departments and the marketing department)?
- Do you work with a framework?
- Do you think it is possible to come up with a framework?
- How do you agree on a theme for the event?
- How do you set milestones?
- What challenges are usually coming up when organizing the event?

Lessons learned from last year:
- What major challenges did you have in the past?
- How did you evaluate the event after the show?
- What are the differences to this year's event?
- Do you see any changes in visitor's expectations and tastes?

Skills needed to organize the event:
- What educational background do you have?
- How did you get involved with the event?
- Is there a typical workday for you?
- What makes a good/bad day for you?
- Do you have a piece of advice?

Post event interview:
- What was the outcome of the event?
- Did you change anything during the event as opposed to the planning part?
- What other challenges did arise during the event?
- With regards to the stages of an event, what would you change during:
  o The research stage
  o The design stage?
  o The planning stage?
  o The actual event?
  o The evaluation of the event?
- Where do you see more potential for the event?
- In your opinion, how many people came to the event?
- What was the best feedback you received during the event?
- What was the worst feedback you got?

- How did you personally like the exhibition?
- What was your most valued lesson during the event?

Appendix 5: Participant Observation

"Exactly how does one go about conducting observation? Werner and Schoepfle (1987, as cited in Angrosino & DePerez, 2000) focus on the process of conducting observations and describe three types of processes:

1. The first is *descriptive observation*, in which one observes anything and everything, assuming that he/she knows nothing; the disadvantage of this type is that it can lead to the collection of minutiae that may or may not be relevant to the study.

2. The second type, *focused observation*, emphasizes observation supported by interviews, in which the participants' insights guide the researcher's decisions about what to observe. 3. The third type of observation, considered by Angrosino and DePerez to be the most systematic, is *selective observation*, in which the researcher focuses on different types of activities to help delineate the differences in those activities (Angrosono & DePerez, 2000, p.677)" (Kawulich, 2005, p. 11).

"Other researchers have taken a different approach to explaining how to conduct observations.

For example, Merriam (1988) developed an observation guide in which she compiled various

elements to be recorded in field notes. The first of these elements includes the physical environment. This involves observing the surroundings of the setting and providing a written description of the context. Next, she describes the participants in detail. Then she records the activities and interactions that occur in the setting. She also looks at the frequency and duration of those activities/interactions and other subtle factors, such as informal, unplanned activities, symbolic meanings, nonverbal communication, physical clues, and what should happen that has not happened. In her 1998 book, Merriam adds such elements as observing the conversation in terms of content, who speaks to whom, who listens, silences, the researcher's own behaviour and how that role affects those one is observing, and what one says or thinks" (Kawulich, 2005, p. 11).